Praise for *The*

"In *The Remodeling Life*, Paul Winans has written much more than a book about how to succeed in the remodeling business. He's shared a business memoir that draws so openly and honestly on his personal experience that the many insights he presents apply equally well to life and business. Aspiring entrepreneurs in any business will recognize the challenges Winans faced and benefit not only from his solutions but also from his thoughtfully reflective approach over the long learning curve that is the default path to success. I wish I'd had this book forty years ago when I was starting my own company."

> — SAL ALFANO, remodeling industry writer, educator, and editor

"Paul Winans is an icon of the remodeling industry. His experience ranges from successfully running his and his wife Nina's own remodeling firm for three decades, serving as President of the National Association of the Remodeling Industry, to being a sought-after speaker for industry events and an author for industry trade journals including *Remodeling*, through which I first met Paul over two decades ago. For many years now Paul has also sought to graciously give back to the industry through his work with Remodelers Advantage and as a consultant to remodeling firms. He's seen it all, learning firsthand from his own mistakes and successes. And now, in *The Remodeling Life*, he offers his wisdom through an easy read, including real-life anecdotes from his own experiences. If you are a seasoned remodeling professional, or just starting out in the business, you owe it to yourself, your family, and your clients to devote two hours to reading this book!"

> —RICK STRACHAN, longtime former publisher of *Remodeling*, *JLC*, and other leading industry media brands

"Paul is a dynamic and insightful businessman who can cut through to the underlying issues and know how to resolve challenges at hand. In today's world, a lot of people claim they are experts. Paul has the battle scars from his struggles, challenges, and successes to back his claims. In his book, *The Remodeling Life*, he shares a lifetime of experience so others don't have to suffer the same pains. Paul's insights into all aspects of remodeling are beneficial whether you've recently started your business or whether you're a seasoned veteran; this book is a must read! I've had the pleasure of knowing Paul for fifteen years. Reading Paul's book reminded me of his contribution to the successful growth of my company. To this day, I hold onto the lessons he's shared with me."

— TODD JACKSON, President, Jackson Design & Remodeling

"Paul is an amazing individual, mentor, and coach, who continues to make a positive difference in my life. Not only did he help me grow personally, he also helped make our company even better. Paul's experience as outlined in his book, *The Remodeling Life*, sharing the various stages of company growth accompanied by the challenges Paul (and Nina) faced, really resonated with me. I am so pleased Paul is able to share his wisdom through his book, continuing to make a positive difference in people's lives—priceless!"

— HERB LAGOIS, Lagois Design Build Renovate

"As Paul points out in *The Remodeling Life*, it is often the owner or owners that are the biggest obstacle to a company achieving great success. Too often we (I included) feel strongly something is true and then proceed to make the same mistakes over and over again without realizing that we are falling into the same trap repeatedly or without reexamining longheld beliefs. Reading this book should help others see those mistakes and learn from them. It should also help create the habit of asking questions, measuring and monitoring results, and instilling continuous improvement into a receptive organization. Developing these good habits can help accelerate a company's prosperity and advance its ability to move to the next level.

"This book also points out how important it is to have a key manager on your team that you can commiserate with, learn from, and strategize with. The member trusted in this case was Nina, his wife, and undoubtedly it helped them become better as a company. Key manager or managers are integral for going from a practice style business to a professionally managed business."

— TY MELTON, President, Melton Design Build

"In his book, *The Remodeling Life: A Journey from Laggard to Leader,* Paul Winans captures your attention quickly with his heartfelt humility, recounting his various successes and struggles as an owner of a construction business. I was quickly drawn into this book, feeling a sense of camaraderie as I compared my own life in business—my own experience—to Paul's. *The Remodeling Life* clearly outlines pitfalls we all face in running a business and the simple steps we can take to make that business thrive.

"Whether you are new to business ownership or a seasoned construction veteran, Paul's writing provides a sense of peace with the past, fellowship for the present, and strategies to guide your future."

— TOM MITCHELL, Owner, Mitchell Construction Group, Inc., Facilitator for Remodelers Advantage

"Paul has expertly captured the essence of gaining experience and the necessity to adapt to the realities of life in our remodelling world … a world that is also regularly subject to the broader impact of economic ups and downs beyond our control.

"I certainly hope that our remodeling colleagues all over the world take the opportunity to read *The Remodeling Life.* If they do, they will learn in advance some things they may find on the road ahead but mostly I think they will learn that they are not alone.

"It was Paul's story that helped build my belief that I would be able to one day sell my own business. I did that and my wife and I are now happily and comfortably retired."

— PETER SHANDS, CGR CAPS, Founder, Professional Home Improvements, Canberra, Australia

"Many companies have 'lessons learned' files. But why wait 15 to 20 years and have many hard knock experiences to get the answers? Paul Winans has brilliantly shared 'lessons learned' and 'solutions applied' in *The Remodeling Life* that will jump-start any new company and propel an existing one into a profitable venture. I am grateful that Paul shared his experience so that for many generations his wisdom will be heard."

— TIM FALLER, Senior Consultant, Remodelers Advantage

"In the construction business, you can choose from among many different paths. Some will take you straight over a cliff. A few can lead to long-term emotional satisfaction and financial success. I was fortunate, because we worked in the same metro area and met regularly in a long-lived builders' association, to be able to watch Nina and Paul Winans travel their particular road to success with determination, courage, and integrity.

"Now I have had the pleasure of reading Paul's humble, clear, and instructive account of that journey. His story of his and Nina's life as remodelers comes in a small package. But it is full of big ideas and candid accounts of mistakes made and lessons learned. In his book, *The Remodeling Life,* we are fortunate to have Paul sharing his hard-earned knowledge with us."

— DAVID GERSTEL, veteran builder and author of
Running A Successful Construction Company, and
*Nail Your Numbers: A Path to Skilled Construction
Estimating and Bidding*

"Distilling the complex into the simple takes someone with a depth of experience, maturity, and intellect. Paul has done it for years for the betterment of the remodeling industry and he does it in *The Remodeling Life.* A must-read for those serious about improving their remodeling business."

— BRUCE CASE, President and CEO, Case Design/
Remodeling, Inc.

"Paul Winans, a noted and notable figure in the remodeling industry for 30 years, has written a personal book about the struggles he and his partner-wife, Nina, learned and grew from as they built their remodeling company to sell in 2007.

"As both a personal and professional friend for most of those 30 years, I have watched Paul grow into a calm, funny, and mature leader. He wasn't always that way: as a younger man he was fierce and determined to succeed; he got wiser as he learned the hard way from his mistakes.

"He details the significant lessons learned through interesting stories and tidbits about his experiences. Readers of *The Remodeling Life* may well see themselves in his travails—by learning from Paul's mistakes many can circumvent some of the obstacles and pain to become the calm and mature leader they desire to be much earlier!

"Make no mistake, however, of the vital role Nina played in the company success. His dedication to Nina reads 'To Nina: you made it possible,' and after reading Paul's book I look forward to reading Nina's.

"Don't reinvent the wheel—read this book and learn from a master remodeler and a master human being."

> — JUDITH MILLER, financial consultant to national
> remodelers, facilitator with Remodelers Advantage, and
> author of *The Remodelers ULTIMATE Guide to QB Pro*

"*The Remodeling Life* is a treasure trove of crucial business guidance assembled through field tested trial and a lot of errors. While it's useful to any customer service industry, the application to remodeling is crystal clear. Winans's writing style is direct and economical and his lessons will save a small business owner millions in lost profits. Mandatory reading for every remodeling company owner."

> — CHIP DOYLE, co-author, *Selling to Homeowners
> the Sandler Way*

"Paul learned from every mistake he made... and got better professionally and became a better human being in the meantime. Paul offers hope and actions to take in dark periods, and cautious optimism when the good times finally roll around in the fiscal cycles businesses commonly experience. *The Remodeling Life* is a good book to read for anyone in any career!"

— **IRIS HARRELL, Founder, Harrell Remodeling**

"They say firsthand experience is one of the best ways to learn, and *The Remodeling Life* certainly speaks to a solid foundation for Paul. His mastery as a coach/ trainer, teacher, and facilitator to the remodeling industry was forged out of his many decades of real life experiences. Paul was my first facilitator at Remodelers Advantage and has continued to guide me on my own personal growth path for almost 15 years since, I will always be most grateful."

— **SCOTT WOOTTON, President,**
www.KawarthaLakesConstruction.com

"Paul's council has been instrumental in growing and developing our remodeling company. He combines wisdom and insight with humility and compassion in a way not found in our industry. He's a true titan of our industry."

— **JEREMY MARTIN, Principal,**
Risher Martin Fine Homes

"Through his time as a consultant to our company, Paul Winans has played a critical role in helping us become a stronger and more profitable business.

"Full of hard-earned wisdom and practical advice, *The Remodeling Life* is a 'must read' for any remodeling business owner who wants to build a better company and build a better life.

"Even after four years of working with Paul on a regular basis, I found myself making notes and creating lists of things to put into practice as I read his book. It is topical, practical, and relevant. I will keep it on the shelf and refer back to it regularly."

— **KYLE L. LISSACK, President, Pinemar, Inc.**

"I have known Paul Winans for over twenty years, and he has been my business coach for the last ten. After talking with Paul monthly for a decade, he has become not only a mentor but also a good friend. Paul has helped me transform my business from a struggling enterprise that produced beautiful projects for no profit to a consistent, robust vehicle to help me achieve my business and personal goals. He has shown remarkable patience as I slowly learned to get out of my own way, and I have provided him with plenty of 'inspiration' for articles over the years. Paul thoughtfully shares his experience and insights in *The Remodeling Life*. It is a great resource for anyone in the construction industry or running a small business."

> — **WRIGHT MARSHALL, President,**
> **Revival Construction, Inc.**

"Working in remodeling for the past two decades, I have met many individuals who help guide our company along a path towards realizing our potential. Only a handful have meant as much to me as Paul Winans. His insight into the heart of the business, our people, has helped mentor, guide, and inspire our entire organization, both individually and collectively, towards realizing the highest successes in our industry.

"Paul has a unique approach, speaking from his heart and from his depth of experiences, to create relatable advice that our team can understand and incorporate into their professional as well as personal lives. *The Remodeling Life* synthesizes our conversations and his style incredibly well and will stay within easy reach as a reference manual for as long as I own a company. I believe Paul truly finds joy in helping others succeed."

> — **GREGORY HARTH, President, Harth Builders**

THE REMODELING LIFE

A Journey from Laggard to Leader

How to Build a
Business That Works for You!

PAUL L. WINANS

PUBLISHED BY SECOND HALF PRESS · ASHLAND, OREGON

The Remodeling Life:
A Journey from Laggard to Leader
by Paul L. Winans

Published by Second Half Press, Ashland, Oregon

Book design: booksavvystudio.com

Library of Congress Control Number: 2019909114

ISBN: 978-0-578-52519-8
First Edition

Printed in the United States of America

To Nina:
you made it possible.

Contents

Foreword

IN ALMOST THREE DECADES at Remodelers Advantage Inc., I've had the opportunity to know many successful business owners—most of them owners of remodeling companies. Those who have realized the highest levels of success in remodeling know that reaching these peaks requires humility, strength of character, empathy, and the ability to stand up for oneself. Talking to and connecting with these passionate individuals is a thrill for me and I learn so much from every conversation.

After all, running a remodeling company is not an easy road. There are many moving pieces to track and control. One must deal with personalities in employees, clients, and trade contractors, which can cause headaches. Outside influences can be a challenge as well, with the recent labor shortage being one example. But the feeling of accomplishment in recreating a home, knowing that the client is delighted, and that you did it all while creating a lovely life for your family and your employees while delivering a profit to the company, is fantastic. Even better is the knowledge that this work will live and provide happiness for decades.

However, building a business that consistently delivers this result is difficult to do on one's own. Most smart remodelers look for help.

And many find Paul Winans.

Paul is certainly the right person to turn to for advice on running a great remodeling company. He did it for many years and, to add to both the blessing and the challenge, he did it with his wife, Nina. Few people know the trials of remodeling better than he does. Not only did Paul gain a depth of experience from running his own company, he also worked with Remodelers Advantage as a facilitator for our Roundtables program for nearly 20 years, gaining the respect and friendship of hundreds of remodelers in the process.

As one of our most popular facilitators, Paul helped guide our members through the journey of business-building—a journey that encompasses employee issues, hiring failures, unhappy clients, fantastic projects, money-making jobs, money-losing mistakes, and the highest highs to the the lowest lows. Paul used his straightforward and honest approach to help these members develop business strategies while they learned to get out of their own way as they grew. He taught and exemplified leadership to each of our members.

This depth of experience is one of the reasons that this book is so good. Paul shares his successes as well as his failures in a way that demonstrates his understanding of what remodelers face every day. Believe me, you'll recognize yourself in many of his stories.

If you want to find out what it really takes to build a strong, profitable remodeling company, it's always best to listen first to someone who has done it himself. Paul Winans is your man.

—Victoria Downing,
President, Remodelers Advantage, Inc.

Preface

Meaningful Mistakes Make
The Most Meaningful Lessons

THIS BOOK IS the distillation of a half-century of experience in the art, science, and commerce of home building, renovating, and remodeling.

The urge to build and fix things appears to have been baked into my DNA. As a four-year-old, I squandered many hours of playtime sitting on a berm of earth between our home and the next, watching transfixed as a contractor renovated that entire house from the foundation to the chimney. One day I got up the nerve to ask him if I could help. He chuckled. "You come see me when you're a little older." Eleven years later, when I was fifteen and had my working papers, I did just that and he hired me.

Thus I hammered my first nail as a carpenter's apprentice on New York's Long Island in the 1960s, when I was still in high school. My father had a similar story to tell. He bought his first car in 1929 when he was fourteen, learned how to repair it, and went on to spend most of his working life as a parts manager for Volkswagen. A great-uncle had been a shipbuilder on Long Island, following in the footsteps of his father, who was a merchant sailor during the Civil War.

After college, my wife, Nina, and I moved to the San Francisco Bay Area where we built and ran a remodeling business for thirty years. We sold it in 2007 and semiretired to southern Oregon where we became customers, having our home completely remodeled and landscaped.

For the past three decades, I've traveled the country participating in industry organizations and events and speaking at trade conferences. For the past ten or so years, I've been consulting for owners of companies that are struggling or in need of a tune-up.

If all that qualifies me as an expert, I got that status by managing to survive in a business that is endlessly complex, highly sensitive to economic booms and busts, and often fickle. When times are good, you're a genius, a stunning success. When the bubble bursts, as it does now and then, it can become a relentless, unforgiving grind just to keep the doors open. A 2017 study by the Joint Center for Housing Studies of Harvard University that tracked homeowner improvement and repair spending in the US found that it shrank between 2007 and 2011—The Great Recession—by 20 percent, making it one of the hardest-hit and longest-suffering business segments.

Like many remodeling company owners and managers, I got my start by aiming to be a first-class craftsperson. My first role model was my father. He was always fixing or making things. When a neighbor cut down a tree, orphaning three baby squirrels, he built a cage and we raised them until they were old enough to be released back into the wild. He made my brother and me a wooden go-cart with lawnmower wheels.

For my mother, he made from scratch a bas-relief wall

hanging of an American bald eagle, jigsawing a piece of plywood into a plaque, sculpting the eagle out of plaster of Paris, and then painting and gilding it with gold leaf. I spent hours watching him, fascinated by how things worked and went together.

After four years of college, I spent several one-year stints working in or running woodshops. Wherever I worked, I often found myself thinking about ways to run the place better. When I had a good, well-formed idea, I'd share it with the foreman or owner. Sometimes my youthful insights were appreciated, but more often than not they were dismissed or ignored. I became frustrated enough that working for myself was the only option.

Like most people in this field, I had no conscious ambition to build a business. I was so naive and idealistic that when Nina suggested I should be marking up our costs, it sounded like she was encouraging me to cheat! As I became more proficient and began to attract more work, I hired a friend to help, but recoiled the first time he addressed me as "Boss."

"We're friends," I scolded. "I don't want to be anybody's boss!" It was the early 1970s and I was a member of a generation that was all about challenging the establishment and leveling hierarchies.

When an opportunity came up that I couldn't resist—to build a house from the foundation up—I was annoyed to find that I'd have to get a contractor's license from the city. The process struck me as a waste of time and money, just to get a piece of paper to prove what I already knew.

I didn't think of myself as running a business. I was just building a house that would stand the test of time. The challenge was too tantalizing to pass up, so I grumbled my way through the red tape.

Our company's first office was a corner of the dining room. I scoffed at the notion that we should pay to rent a real office outside the home. But when our accountant told us we'd never be a real business until we had a real office, we capitulated and discovered how nice it is to be able to leave work at work—mostly!

In the early years, I resisted the idea that we needed to be selling our work. Selling was what happened on used-car lots. As comfortable as I had become working with wood and nails, those skills could not prepare me for managing, leading, and inspiring employees, or for working with customers.

Every lesson I learned along the way about running a complex business I initially resisted or struggled with, or was the result of a mistake. In spite of it all, Nina and I eventually established an enterprise that allowed us to take real vacations knowing our employees could be trusted to keep our clients happy and the company profitable. We built a reputation so solid that we were able to sell the firm when it came time to retire. That's the short version of a long journey.

Within this slender volume you will find a toolbox of techniques, tactics, strategies, insights, and suggestions on how to build, manage, and monetize a successful remodeling business. Some will seem obvious, others may challenge you, and some could be the key that solves a serious dilemma. I've tried to organize the material in such a way that you can dip your toe in anywhere and find some nugget of wisdom or perhaps just confirmation that you're on the right track.

The future for our industry looks bright. An August 2016 piece on NPR's *Morning Edition* reported, "There's a home renovation boom, but good luck finding a contractor." Now is the time to learn your lessons and make your mistakes, while the sun shines, so you'll be ready for the next inevitable economic storm.

This book is divided into three sections. In Part One, you'll read about how to remodel yourself without being overwhelmed by your business. In Part Two, you'll learn about how to build the team of employees who'll bring tears of joy to your eyes. Finally, in Part Three, you'll get insights about to have your business work for you. With this knowledge you will be more likely to make fewer mistakes and to experience the success you deserve, no matter what the future holds.

—Paul L. Winans
Ashland, Oregon, 2019

THERE ARE NO SECRETS TO SUCCESS.
IT IS THE RESULT OF PREPARATION, HARD WORK,
AND LEARNING FROM FAILURE.

— General Colin L. Powell

PART I

First, Remodel Yourself

CHAPTER 1

Get Out of Your Own Way

OVER THE PAST DECADE or so, I've met, addressed, or worked with hundreds of people like yourself who are wrestling with a problem. The typical opening remark of remodelers I've met in my consulting practice is: "I'm stuck."

"What's the obstacle?"

The most common refrain: "It's my people."

What follows is a litany of complaints and expressions of frustration with employees who show up late, communicate or follow directions poorly, quit without notice—all the maddening behaviors that all business owners have to deal with but which are especially disruptive in a field like ours. And, of course, "You just can't find good people these days." It's all true, and to one degree or another it always has been.

It's the rare owner who identifies the person who is the biggest problem—themselves. I learned this the hard way over three decades, growing what began as youthful passion for carpentry into a healthy, profitable, family-owned remodeling business in Oakland, California, with revenue of about $3 million a year.

For much of that journey, "my people" would have been

my default explanation when struggling to meet deadlines or payrolls. It took me a long time to comprehend that I was reaping what I had sown. I was ultimately responsible for the behavior of those I had hired and trained.

As an apprentice carpenter in the 1960s, my first boss—a seasoned craftsman with calloused hands—offered object lessons I would come to appreciate only after years of experience. He never complained. Whatever wasn't going right, he said, "We'll deal with it." He never raised his voice or lost his temper. He was wisdom incarnate.

Also, he was very private. We never talked about anything but work, and then only what was necessary to get the task done. At the end of the day, I hopped on my bike and rode home. At the end of the week he handed me the envelope with my pay in it, down to the penny, and I wouldn't see or speak to him until Monday morning. We never talked about how each of us had spent his weekend. He'd make an occasional encouraging remark about my skills progress but not much beyond that.

Employees Or Comrades?

Fast forward to the early 1980s, when our business was still relatively young. On Fridays, I would arrive at the job site at quitting time with a case of beer. For an hour or so we'd all sit around gossiping, telling stories about ourselves and each other, enjoying the bonhomie of comrades in arms.

I regarded "my people" as comrades. I wanted them to feel a part of our business family, to know I valued them as more than just guys I paid to do a job. I thought it was a way to establish loyalty and community.

The problem with this approach became apparent when it was time to correct, discipline, or fire someone who mistook my friendly Fridays for permission to show up late, take unscheduled days off, ask for pay advances, and all the other incursions that blur the boundary between employer and employee. How do you fire someone who, beer bottle in hand, has shared that he is going through an ugly divorce and can't pay his lawyer? Or someone who's told you about

I was ultimately responsible for the behavior of those I had hired and trained.

an aging parent who needs care they can't afford? Or someone with whom you have overshared details about your own personal life that subtly undermine your status as the leader?

In the years that followed, I made halting progress toward running a more professional business, learning how to be more strict and beating myself up when I slipped. The epiphany, when it finally came, was in retrospect so obvious: we were running a business, not an employment agency. The purpose of that business was to make money doing great work for people who wanted to pay for it. The ultimate goal was to provide meaning and create opportunities for ourselves and our family that would not otherwise be possible. Simple in theory, but it took many years for that sort of thinking to become automatic. I had to remodel my assumptions.

Carpentry Catnip

The second epiphany had to do with the allure of taking on projects that provided meaning to me personally—creative, challenging, visible—but that failed to make money that would sustain the business. The more complex the project, the more glorious or attractive, the more likely I was to go for it without first kicking the tires.

The project that triggered this epiphany was carpentry catnip: restoring the library in a Mediterranean Revival mansion that is today home of the Montalvo Arts Center in Saratoga, California, about fifty miles south of San Francisco. Villa Montalvo was built by James D. Phelan, a political leader who had inherited from his father a fortune made during the California Gold Rush. Phelan died in 1930, leaving the property to the state to be maintained as a public park and an art center.

Over the next fifty years and multiple renovations, the once-magnificent library had been butchered so utterly that the job essentially involved recreating it from old photographs. It was all carpentry and cabinetry work—materials and labor.

When you're a remodeling company and all you're doing is carpentry work, it's hard to earn a reasonable return. But it was a marquee project that satisfied my interest in the restoration of historical landmarks. You can learn a lot about carpentry by studying how it was done back when the choice of materials was limited and the tools were more basic.

We put four people on the job, which was about eighty miles away from our office—too far to ask them to commute. We bought a van and used it to ferry the crew to and from the site each day. When it was all done, we had some trophy photographs to show for our effort but not enough profit to justify the distraction from more lucrative and convenient work. And it led to another all-carpentry job restoring old bunkhouses in a state park on the Pacific Coast, also a long drive from home base.

At some point in this process, it began to dawn on me that I might have become one of those entrepreneurs who business guru and *The E-Myth* author Michael E. Gerber once described as "technicians with an entrepreneurial seizure." These projects satisfied my artistic sensibilities and the satisfaction of breathing life into history. They did not enhance our profitability or the stability of the company.

The hardest lesson was yet to come, in 1990–91 when the economy was in retreat and unemployment was rising. We had no work to speak of when an architect gave us a referral for a job that was worth $140,000. It, too, was a distance from our office, but we really needed it. In the process, I blew right past a bunch of warning signs.

First, the architect said he was handing the project off to take on a bigger job. I should have asked why, because the answer might have saved me a lot of grief. The house was in a city where we'd never worked, didn't know the subcontractors, and had no relationship with the city building department.

When we met with the couple who owned the house, the husband never once made eye contact. His wife had worked in an architectural office and let us know that she thought she was an expert—nobody's fool. It was a cost-plus not-to-exceed bid, with a bonus if we brought it in under budget.

It was a headache from the get-go. We put our best person in charge, but as the visiting team it was a struggle navigating the permit process and finding suitable subcontractors. The good ones were busy and the rest were desperate. Nevertheless, we got it done, brought it in under budget, and presented our invoice for the $5,000 bonus. The customer ignored it. We filed a mechanic's lien, which they also ignored.

About a year had passed when one day the mail brought a certified letter—notice that they were suing us for the full price of the job. They had hired an expert who'd put the work under a microscope, finding every conceivable variation between our proposal and invoices, and a few that didn't exist. The wife, meanwhile, began a campaign to discredit us among our clients and architects. She also made harassing phone calls to our office posing as a workers' compensation investigator. To shorten a long, sad tale, we ended up in arbitration and lost, badly. We had to repay the customer $40,000 over two years, right when money was tightest.

There were other bad calls, jobs with warning signs I failed to heed. But I did eventually learn the lesson, watching projects we didn't win go south for other companies.

We became more discerning about those we shouldn't have gotten before they went south for us. One in particular was for a couple, of which one was clearly making all the decisions. It was hard to schedule meetings, but still I pushed through the process, got it designed and priced, and got the contract signed.

Then I got to thinking. They had never worked the way we did, figuring everything out on the front end so that any change orders would not come out of our pocket. They had only ever worked with one other contractor on a time and materials basis. The deciding spouse would come home from work, see what had been done that day, and decide to make changes. The warning signs were now clearer to me.

So I called the customer and said, "I've given it a lot of thought, and in the end I'm not sure we're the right fit for this project." To my surprise, she said, "Oh, thank you, thank you, Paul! We were feeling the same thing."

So we tore up the contract. It may have been the most money we ever made by not doing a job.

ASK YOURSELF THESE QUESTIONS

1. Have you described your company as "a family"
   to your employees?

   _____

   _____

   _____

2. Have you done a project that was attractive as a
   challenge but could not be done profitably?

   _____

   _____

   _____

3. Have you taken on a project that just didn't feel
   right because you "really needed the work"?

   _____

   _____

   _____

Most of us can answer "Yes" to at least one of these
questions. What you do from this point on is up to
you and no one else.

CHAPTER 2

Measure Twice,
Hire Once

HIRING THE RIGHT PEOPLE is always a challenge, and uniquely so when your business cycle is subject to the whims of weather and economic conditions. In the first years of my experience, I lucked out by finding a couple of good people early on. It took a lot longer to figure out what went wrong when subsequent hires would wash out.

If I was looking for a lead carpenter or a production manager, I'd interview the finalists by explaining how the company was organized and run, describing clients and projects we had worked on, and laying out my expectations for performance. That would take about fifteen minutes, during which the applicant would sit there listening and nodding, with an occasional "Uh-huh."

Finally, I'd wind up my speech by asking, "So, any questions?"

It frustrated me that so few had the kinds of probing questions that would have suggested they were listening and thinking. Some of them may have had a lot of good questions, but looking back on it I'm sure they'd forgotten them by the time I was done, or perhaps I had just worn them out.

My awakening as an employer was sparked by Darrel, one of the yardmen at the local lumber supplier, a family-owned business that had been around a long time. Like me, Darrel was in his thirties and eager to please. He looked at my order ticket one day and asked, "So, what are you using this for?"

I was startled at first. What's it to you, I thought? But after a couple of times of his having good suggestions for alternative materials, I was glad when he said, "You might want to try this. It's less expensive." Or, "This might be easier to work with." He never pushed one product over another, but his suggestions were typically spot on. In time he was the only person in the yard I'd have pick my orders. When the opportunity came up, I offered him a job. Darrel ended up working for us for more than twenty-five years.

That experience convinced me to get professional advice and read some books. That eventually led to a full remodeling of our hiring process. Instead of talking about the company, I spent almost all of the interview process asking questions that were specific and challenging.

"Let's say you're the project manager on a large remodel and you get a call from the job site informing you that one of our trucks has just driven over two prize rose bushes belonging to a neighbor. You can hear the neighbor swearing loudly in the background. How do you deal with that?"

Or, "The water main has just broken at a job site and a torrent is flowing downhill into the customer's garage. The clients are out of town. Write the message you'd send letting them know what's happened and what you're going to do about it."

That process eliminated many candidates for a variety of reasons. Some failed to suggest the first step—letting us know in the office—and said they would go ahead and try to solve it on their own. Others were focused on protecting themselves and the company from blame. We also studied the messages we asked them to write for spelling, tone, clarity, grammar, and how long they took to write it.

The most important thing I learned?

S-L-O-W D-O-W-N.

If it doesn't feel good at the interview, it's likely not going to get any better.

It's a theme that came to inform everything we did. In the case of hiring, it meant avoiding the mistake of employing someone in spite of what seemed at the time to be small doubts: "Well, we can deal with that when he's on the job," or, "It's not a big deal that this guy is a little over-eager. We could use some energy."

If you don't address your doubts or listen to your instincts during the interview process and hire someone because you "don't have time" to get it right, the price could turn out to be steep. There's the cost of carrying someone who may not be productive or may even be disruptive for weeks, maybe months, because you're that short-handed. And then you have to go through the process of hiring all over again. If it doesn't feel good at the interview, it's likely not going to get any better.

Measure twice, cut once. You won't have time to fix it later.

CHAPTER 3

Expect The Unexpected

I T WAS A BEAUTIFUL sunny California afternoon in 1991. I was sitting on a rock at the Berkeley Marina, looking at the Golden Gate Bridge. This was a new ritual, getting away from home for an hour or so to give Nina a rest from my relentless moaning about how bad things were. I usually brought one or two of our sons with me, but on this day I was alone and sank into a funk.

"What did I do to deserve this?" I muttered. We'd been in business almost fifteen years and things had been going well. Home values were rising fast, providing equity that owners were borrowing against to remodel and increase the value even more. And then the economy went into a stall.

Although mortgage rates had come down from historical highs of the 1980s (above 15 percent for 30-year fixed-rate mortgages!), they had gotten stuck at around 10 percent. Fueled in part by the fear that they'd start rising again, residential investment as a percentage of GDP cratered. On top of all that, California was getting clobbered by the US Department of Defense's Base Realignment and Closure program. More than 93,000 Californians who were on the DOD's payroll lost their jobs—more than the rest of the country combined.

In our little patch of this apocalypse, clients were hitting the brakes on half-finished projects, contracts were going unsigned, leads were elusive, and cash flow dried up. It shouldn't have come as a shock because the East Coast had been hit by that recession first.

Someone with more experience would have seen the tsunami coming. This was my first exposure to the potential damage of economic cycles. Up until then I thought I had this remodeling business all figured out. Now we had essentially no work, few qualified leads, and a file drawer full of mouldering estimates.

To make matters worse, we had just bought, remodeled, and moved into our own building, an investment that would take years to recoup in good times. Our costs had gone up and our gross revenue was down by a third. To keep our people busy, we put them to work over-improving the new office. We used some of our savings and credit lines to do some projects on our home, too.

We ran out of money right around the time we ran out of in-house projects. I was worried we would lose our key folks, people we'd spent years nurturing who were accustomed to working with our processes.

Find The Partners In Your People

As she has so often in our shared career, Nina got us out of our funk by looking with a practical eye at how we were operating. She suggested that we continue our usual Monday morning progress-report meetings, which included all our employees. That weekly meeting had become a staple of the company by then and would remain so until the day we sold it.

Now, instead of talking to each other and commiserating, Nina and I shared with our crew our marketing efforts, what sales activity there was, what leads were coming in, appointments I had coming up with prospective clients, estimating activity—the works. We paid them for that hour as well.

Nina correctly understood that giving our most valued employees this information demonstrated that we weren't sitting around waiting for a miracle, that we were in it for keeps and we were determined to ride out the storm. As a result, they were more inclined to sacrifice with us.

This practice also relieved a lot of the stress I was feeling about being a failure and letting other people down. We heard the trade gossip about how tough it was at other companies, as well as opportunities we might otherwise have missed. We became more of a professional community than just a company with bosses and workers.

Some of our people had side jobs. We encouraged them to hire their coworkers to help pick up the slack. When we got a call for a job that was so small we couldn't charge enough to cover the cost, we referred them to our employees, playing an ad hoc agency role.

We offered employees the option to take some of their vacation time early. The company had a generous profit-sharing plan. That year we had none, but we gave each person a Costco gift basket as a way of saying, "If we could, we would.

And when we can, we will."

One of the most important lessons I learned during that experience was that bad news is best served fresh. As many business owners do, we could have tried to keep up the appearance of prosperity and confidence until the well was dry. One day without notice we'd have to lay everybody off and maybe even have to fold the company. Instead, we leveraged our relationships with our key people to spread the misery for a common cause: survival.

Bad news is best served fresh. It was a tactic we had already been applying to handling client expectations. Our standard operating procedure was to respond to clients' requests for information, estimates, or other concerns by a specific date and time. We made it a priority to keep our promises. Even if we had nothing to report, we reported that. If it was bad news, we made sure they heard it from us first, in a timely fashion. Otherwise it's human nature that people will suspect they're being kept in the dark about something important, becoming anxious and making negative assumptions.

That recession helped remodel my sense of purpose and how I perceived my role as the leader. I had to accept that I didn't have everything figured out and embrace the notion that I didn't always need to. It also taught me the profound truth expressed in that familiar saying about luck being what happens when preparation meets opportunity.

When Preparation Meets Opportunity

We had toughed out the worst of it—about nine months— when one Friday afternoon in the fall of 1991 I found myself sitting at my tidy desk in our beautiful, over-remodeled office and shop jotting down numbers, trying to figure out how much longer we could hold out. I was also checking on preparations for our first open house, scheduled for the following week. We'd spread the word, sent out a mailing, and hoped for a good turnout that would lead to some much-needed new business.

That Saturday, a small grass fire broke out in the nearby hills overlooking Oakland, Berkeley, and San Francisco Bay. Firefighters knocked it down the same day and declared it out. The next day, some stray embers rekindled the bone-dry brush. Then a windstorm fanned the flames into a roaring monster that rampaged through one desirable neighborhood after another, leaving behind scorched earth, charred tree trunks, and blackened chimneys. By the time the sun rose the next morning, a Monday, more than 3,000 homes, apartments, and condos and their contents had been incinerated, a total inflation-adjusted loss of nearly $3 billion. Twenty-five people died and 150 were injured.

This tragedy in our backyard was, to paraphrase Winston Churchill, not the end of our travails, but it was the beginning of the end. Had I known in advance about the downturn in the economy we might have held off buying that building. It was a decision I had often second-guessed at the time but one that, in the end, confirmed my instincts.

We were able to pick it up at a bargain price because the commercial real estate market was in the tank at the time. Buying it was a risk but it felt like the right move to step up our game, to position ourselves as a solid, established company with a visible, professional footprint. Had we waited until business recovered, the price might well have been out of reach.

So when the recovery finally began, we found ourselves better prepared than most smaller companies to compete. On the Friday before the weekend of the Oakland fire, we had been worried about booking just one decent-sized job to keep us going a little longer.

The Monday after the fire, billions of dollars worth of work were suddenly up for grabs. On the other hand, we found ourselves competing for it with an invasion of big contractors and independent operators chasing the cornucopia of insurance money about to pour into rebuilding the burned-over neighborhoods. There was so much work I was confident business would pick up as soon as the fire trucks were gone and the roadblocks taken down.

CHAPTER 4

My Divine Dissatisfaction

M Y OPTIMISM PROVED PREMATURE. A full year passed before we finally broke ground on our first insurance rebuild. Until then, much of my time was spent doing insurance estimates for fees that helped with cash flow but that were a poor return for a week's worth of work. During that time I prepared about thirty complicated, detailed proposals that involved protracted negotiations—enough paper to fill a file drawer. But the actual jobs were elusive.

Our market swarmed with new competitors. At the top end were much bigger companies that, had the economy been better, might otherwise have been busy developing subdivisions. They now trained their sights on the Oakland-Berkeley fire rebuild, which included some sizable condo projects. On the low end, people who had worked for smaller companies and been laid off were now launching start-ups, often with just a pickup truck, a tool case, and one or two projects.

Those homeowners who did want to rebuild often found themselves in drawn-out squabbles with their insurance companies. Others were so traumatized they couldn't think about designing and building a new home. Still others took the insurance money and moved away.

By the time the dust finally settled and the economy had begun picking up, only a few start-ups had survived and the big players were going back to building housing developments. The opportunity to grow our business had finally arrived and we were prepared. While we were physically remodeling the company into our professional shop and offices, I had been remodeling myself.

Sight Preparation

The sense of failure I experienced during the downturn motivated me to rethink how I related to the world. I read self-help books, took personality tests, attended courses and retreats, and listened to Nina. An introvert by nature, I had always avoided networking and hobnobbing. The hour or so it took to attend a Chamber of Commerce lunch was exhausting and the whole time I felt like I ought to have been back at the office finishing an estimate or pricing materials or a hundred other things that needed to be done.

The lesson I finally learned was that preparation is more than nuts and bolts. It requires getting outside your bubble, even if that means the occasional Rotary or Chamber luncheon. But that's just the beginning. What follows are some of the things I started doing that I came to understand are part of being prepared. They seem obvious now, but many business owners I work with have persuaded themselves that they don't have time. They do, but they have to be convinced it'll pay off.

The Easy Stuff

Find out what's happening in business in your community. Read the local business publications. They often report the kind of news that could save you a lot of grief later: bankruptcies, mechanics liens, lawsuits, and so on. You may learn about people who you should avoid doing business with. A subcontractor who is filing mechanics liens is probably going to be cash poor, may be cutting corners, and is more likely to pressure you to get paid before the job is done. You may be surprised, as we once were, to discover that a subcontractor has filed for bankruptcy without bothering to tell us.

Subscribe to a few trade publications such as *Remodeling, Professional Remodeler,* and *Qualified Remodeler.* There are a slew of websites, publications, and blogs that cover niche markets: *Builder,* the *Journal of Light Construction, Green Home Builder, Fine Homebuilding, Walls & Ceilings,* and *Concrete Homes*—something for everyone. Find the ones that seem the most relevant to you and make a habit of taking an hour or so a week to read up on what's happening.

Notice economic mega-trends. When the economy crashed in 2008, it was no surprise to some very alert people who pay attention to things like interest rates, home sales data, unemployment rates, and so on. You don't have to be an economist to know that when home prices start to soften the economy can't be far behind. But you may be surprised to know that every recession since the early 1950s began when unemployment rates had hit a low.

As I write this, the unemployment rate in the US hovers around 4 percent, and at one point was at its lowest in almost half a century. Small wonder that a growing chorus of economists are warning of tough times ahead. At the very least, as the labor pool shrinks, the cost of labor rises, profits are squeezed, prices increase, inflation picks up, the Federal Reserve raises interest rates, and growth slows—all the ingredients for a recession.

The Hard Stuff

I had to learn to be the person who gets out and talks to others in the community. Whether it's the teller at the bank or the person behind the counter at the donut shop, it doesn't cost anything to introduce yourself and use those interactions as opportunities to find out what's going on in the community. How's business? If you hear from a variety of people in different fields that things are slow, that's intelligence that could inform the choices you're making. If everybody's doing great and you aren't, then maybe you need to make some changes.

All those people you meet in the course of everyday life who now are aware of who you are and what you do are potential viral marketers—they now know someone in the construction business who they might mention to a potential client.

Talk to your professional services people. Maybe take your lawyer, your banker, or your accountant to lunch. What do they see happening? What's the future look like? What are they hearing from other people? They're going to be able to give you insights you can't get by staying fixated on your own business.

Knowing how you're doing and what you're planning, these professionals may end up giving you leads or ideas where to get them, or passing your name on to other clients. Don't be afraid to share information about your business. Depending on your level of familiarity with these trusted advisors, it can feel good just to talk about and describe your business to someone who isn't in the trenches with you. Conversations like that can often produce good ideas and revelations.

During the recession of 1990–91, we started reaching out to former clients. We hoped doing so would generate some new business, although that wasn't the pitch. "It's been a couple of years since we worked on your home. How are you enjoying it? Is there anything that needs attention? We're able to offer you service relatively quickly right now." It wasn't my favorite task, but eventually it became part of our process, and we continued the practice even after the economy picked up.

We did get the occasional small fix-it project from making these calls. But where this practice really paid off was in further building relationships with some good clients who, over time, went on to give us several more significant projects. By reminding them of how much we thought of them, we made it hard to forget how much they enjoyed the experience of working with us.

Manage Yourself

The hardest part of remodeling myself was learning to manage my emotions. I'm the type of person who strives for order and perfection. When I saw disorder and imperfection, I could become a terror on a job site. For a time I drove an eight-cylinder GMC Suburban that had a telltale growl you could hear half a block away. I had developed such a reputation that I'm told swearing would break out when employees heard it coming up the street.

I'd get out of the truck with my head already a battlefield of unfinished business, incomplete tasks, and unmet expectations. My father was an old-school parent, stingy with praise and generous with criticism and correction. So that's what I instinctively dealt out when I found material wrappings blowing around in the wind, or a pile of lumber scattered instead of stacked, or tools that weren't being used and should have been back in the shop so somebody else could find them—for Pete's sake!

It took some determination, self-examination, and input from our key people to find a better way. For starters, I had to find something to praise. I might tell the lead carpenter, "The client is so happy with the way you're communicating with them. You're doing a great job. It reinforces in the client's mind how smart they were for hiring us." If the job site was tidy and our people had made sure to carefully protect the floors, I'd make a point of it while talking with the guys on the job. We codified this practice with written comments on cards.

24

Allow Yourself To Be Managed

There were always things to correct or complain about, but I was relieved of the whip by our production manager, Nancy. We agreed that I was no longer permitted to go to a job site without her, and while there I was only permitted to point out the things I was happy about. The only person I could complain to was Nancy, and only in private. She might agree and correct whatever and whomever needed it. But she used her judgment about when was the right time and place.

If my problem was a production issue, Nancy could look at it more objectively. Sometimes she would say, "No, Paul. We're not going to lose money trying to make this perfect. The client's happy and the lead carpenter did what we estimated. Your idea is great. We'll make it part of the process and use it on the next project."

None of this was easy, but in time I came to accept that there were some things I was better at than others. I had once thought it was cool to sit and drink beer on Friday afternoons with my employees, to be one of the guys. Now they were part of our weekly meeting, they were giving us valuable feedback, we were giving them support and encouragement, and we had cemented the ties that bind by surviving the recession together. I couldn't argue with the result, and I wasn't enabling any alcoholics.

Understanding oneself is the essential work of a satisfying life. For me that work was key to the success of our business. I remain an introvert and still strive for perfection and order. But I gradually overcame the self-doubt and lack of confidence I'd felt sitting on a rock by the bay in Berkeley, wondering, "What did I do to deserve this?"

Most of the business people I've met are plagued by the sort of dissatisfaction that only lets you see what could be better and that keeps you from taking satisfaction in what is great. The same is true of people involved in the theater, a passion Nina and I share. There's a connection here that British psychologist Havelock Ellis identified in 1923 in his book *The Dance of Life.* He wrote that dance and architecture were the original forms of art. Dance expressed what was inside the person and "the art of building ... is the beginning of all the arts that lie outside the person."

Understanding oneself is the essential work of a satisfying life.

Martha Graham, the legendary pioneer of modern dance, is credited with a quote that elegantly describes the struggle so many of us can identify with: "No artist is pleased. There is no satisfaction whatever at any time. There is only a queer, divine dissatisfaction, a blessed unrest that keeps us marching and makes us more alive than the others."

CHAPTER 5

Married …With Clients

FAMILY-OWNED REMODELING COMPANIES tend to organize themselves according to rules we associate with our cave-dwelling ancestors. The men hunt and the women cook. Mom and Pop. At least that's how things often start out. Although gender roles have become more fluid over time, the model for the entrepreneurial couple endures and it even has a name: co-entrepreneurial business. The partners are sometimes called "co-preneurs."

Nina and I had known each other since high school, so we became business partners the way many couples do—incrementally and without any sort of plan. By the time we sold the business in 2007, we had clocked more than three decades of experience. Our marriage survived and thrived, we raised and educated three sons, and we were able to semiretire to a city that suited our interests and lifestyle while I pursued a second career as a consultant.

We've often been asked—and I have sometimes wondered—"How'd you do it?" We've heard our share of stories of families that were torn apart by business. Were it possible to sit down with our young selves back in the 1970s,

I'd offer a few lessons learned and a few observations about navigating these treacherous waters.

Learning To Juggle

When I started the business in the 1970s, Nina was at home with our first two children, an infant and a small child. She began, as many partner-mothers do, by using her limited experience as a bookkeeper and then—textbook at her elbow to fill in the gaps in her knowledge—poring over the checkbook, logging invoices and bills, and figuring out payroll taxes.

Our office was an alcove in our dining room where Nina had a desk and I had a counter. We shared a five-drawer file cabinet and the only phone in the house. At first it only took her a couple of hours a week, but the task began to consume more time as the business grew. The ringing of the phone began to define our days, and then our nights, and then it intruded on our Sunday mornings. We bought an answering machine to screen the calls, but I couldn't help worrying that it was something important so I'd end up answering the phone anyway.

Then we had a separate business line installed, but I was like a sight hound spotting a rabbit—nothing could stop me. One Thanksgiving, as we were about to carve the turkey, the business line rang. Nina called out, "Paul, *don't*!" I had to know. It was Thanksgiving. It must be an emergency.

"Hey, Paul, it's Glen. Glad I got ya. Listen, I was going over these invoices for our project and I think I discovered that we overpaid you by a couple grand." Nina and I still laugh about that one today.

When we had a chance to remodel our own home, we were able to free up a room on the first floor—an actual office with a door. But Nina did not have a "real" job. She was still juggling housework and office work. She began to feel she was losing her identity. She wanted to do her part for the business but there was too much going on under one roof, too much overlap between family and work. For me, work was paramount. For Nina, family and home came first.

Getting "Real"

The breakthrough, as mentioned earlier, came when our accountant—always dressed in a suit and tie—made one of his periodic visits to go over our books. More bluntly than we were used to he said, "You realize you're not a real business, right?" My hackles rose. What the hell? "You'll never be a real business until you move your office out of this house."

I felt like I'd been sucker punched. Nina felt like he had discovered the most vulnerable place in her psyche and was poking at it with a sharp stick. After we'd had a few days to digest his critique, we realized he was right. We searched for months until we found the right situation and moved our office into a building that was a twenty-minute drive from home.

Overnight everything became real: we had a real office, we were a real business, Nina had a real job, and we became real business partners. As our children got older and more independent, her role evolved to include administrative and marketing responsibilities.

"For the first time," she recalls, "I worked *with* my husband instead of *for* him. I was proud to identify myself to others as co-owner of a home remodeling firm."

Our Top Five Basic Lessons

1. Find a way to separate home from work.

Having an office a short drive from home provides a valuable transition each morning and night, from spouse to coworker and back again.

If an office in the home is still the best solution, consider giving it a separate entrance. You can create the transition effect by scheduling appointments or errands for first thing in the morning so you leave the house like a professional, freshly showered and dressed to meet the public. When you return, it's straight to the office.

2. Have a clear division of responsibilities.

I handled sales and production and Nina handled administrative and financial duties. There are many permutations possible depending on the temperament and background of the partners. The key element is to make sure each has a well-defined role that suits them.

---

3. Find an activity that takes you away from work on a regular basis

For many years the business was always on my mind. I would show up at home for meals and family occasions, but my head was always elsewhere.

One day I was unexpectedly recruited to participate in a casual softball game. I had played sports in high school and loved baseball, and in spite of all the years that had passed it turned out I was halfway decent. So I joined a league and began to play regularly. At one point I was on three different teams. It was fun, gratifying, good exercise, and it provided a respite from obsessing about the business. It was also liberating to be able to take a break from being the boss for an hour or two and just be one of the guys.

I developed a habit of going for a walk every day for about an hour. I wandered up and down the streets of our neighborhood, or drove somewhere else for a change of scenery. I often took my sons along when they were young. If I spotted a construction site I'd always stop and have a look around, see what the others were up to, and point out interesting things to the kids.

Our youngest was the most resistant. He didn't want to go, dragged his feet along the way, and groused about how bored he was. Fast forward fifteen or twenty years and... guess what? He told us one day that our walks together are some of his most cherished childhood memories!

4. Don't mingle personal and business money.

Nina and I are planners. Each year we did our best to project our revenue and expenses and, based on that, gave ourselves paychecks along with everyone else in the company. If we had a good year, we might get a bonus at the end.

A mistake some owners make is using business cash or credit for purchases like a new car or an ambitious vacation. You risk your employees taking note—they'll remember when it comes time to discuss raises if you'll have to tell them the company can't afford it. As an employer and a leader, you are always on stage and everything you do is being interpreted by those you lead. Your behavior around money in particular tells employees a lot about your commitment to them and to the company.

When business was poor we learned not to use our personal money to fill the gap. This is another common mistake. Once you start taking out equity loans against your house or dipping into a retirement account it's a challenge to find the right moment and the extra cash flow to take it back out. That can create a lot of stress and become a source of resentment in the partnership. It's much harder than you think to "make it up later."

Instead, we built up a line of credit during the flush times when we had robust cash flow and our balance sheet was strong. We didn't use it until we hit a soft patch or a cash-flow gap, as often happens in contracting. The installment payments became just another item on our list of bills each month.

5. Couples should have well-defined long-range goals.

In our case, it became clear early on that our sons would not be joining us as partners, nor would they be taking the business over when it was time for us to retire. In 1998, Nina and I agreed that by the year 2008 we would be living a remodeling company–free life. In the absence of interest from our sons to carry it on, we would either close the doors, sell it to our employees, or possibly find a buyer.

We made it a point to schedule periodic meetings between us to monitor our progress and make any adjustments. If you don't carve that time out and talk about what you want to accomplish personally and as a couple, you won't have the foundation for achieving your goals. Life just happens to you. As Yogi Berra, the New York Yankees catcher who became famous for his malapropisms, is said to have quipped. "If you don't know where you're going, you might not get there."

The decision we made to exit in 2008 fundamentally altered the way we thought about and ran the company. For example, I learned to become less attached to my self-image as the founder-owner of the business. It helped me emotionally when it came time to walk away.

We had hardly ever taken any time off, so we made that a goal and began taking vacations that required leaving the company in the hands of our key people. That also helped prepare us for our permanent departure.

In general, personal goals should drive your business goals, not the other way around. The purpose of being in business is to provide the resources to support your life, your family, and your personal interests. Figuring out what those goals are and how to achieve them as a couple can be nettlesome.

Getting Unstuck

One of the toughest aspects for me was keeping the communication going with Nina. When I got stressed out and was feeling burdened—like there was no one else in the world who had ever been where I was and who could understand what I was dealing with—I tended to shut down. When you're not talking to each other, you end up taking unilateral actions in your marriage or your business that the other partner is expected to support without having had a say. That leads to friction and misunderstanding. When we got stuck we hired a business consultant—a neutral, objective third party to help us sort things out and get synchronized.

In general, personal goals should drive your business goals, not the other way around.

A life, a relationship, a business—they are all works in progress from beginning to end. Nothing is ever "fixed" for good. People grow, goals change, businesses evolve. A healthy partnership at home can make the difference between a business that stutters and a business that hums. And a well-run business can enrich a relationship, as it did ours.

PART II

Remodel Your Team

CHAPTER 6

The Turnover Problem

A FTER MORE THAN TWO DECADES of getting to know, learn from, and consult for remodeling companies, I'd say the most exasperating task—and the focus of one of my most important epiphanies—has been recruiting, hiring, and retaining key people. It's just like herding cats. Turnover tends to be high so it's endless. Doing it well is often the difference between survival and success, between misery and satisfaction.

Send a skilled bookkeeper to just about any type of business and the job will likely get done. An insurance agent switches companies and it's mostly a question of signage and business cards. Remodeling by definition means custom work performed by people who are experienced and often proud specialists in diverse trades, working on or inside the most personal spaces of anxious, inexperienced clients with lofty expectations and financial anxieties. Phew!

Recruiting and retention is the headache that never goes away. It became especially painful for those in the remodeling business after it bottomed out in 2011. During the Great Recession, an estimated two million construction workers hung up their hard hats for good.

Then came an explosive recovery in housing starts—up more than 40 percent by the end of 2012. But residential construction employment essentially flatlined. There were plenty of job openings, thus there was plenty of job hopping.

By 2017, turnover was still running above 20 percent overall, but that number turns out to be misleading when broken down by age groups. A 2017 ADP Workforce Vitality Report found turnover among construction employees aged twenty-four and younger was more than 60 percent and among 25- to 34-year-olds it was 30 percent.

In other words, companies are having to recruit, replace, and train about half of their younger workers, every year! The Center for American Progress (CAP) estimated the cost to employers of replacing low-to-mid-level construction workers at between 15 percent and 20 percent of their annual base pay. That works out to about $6,000 for an entry-level laborer earning $20 an hour and $11,000 for an employee earning $35 an hour. Multiply those numbers by half your younger workers and that's the price of turnover, year in and year out.

"A construction business's greatest value lies in its people," reported CAP, which is a nonpartisan policy institute. "The greatest danger of employee turnover is when companies go on their merry way totally oblivious to what it's costing them."

Worse still, a 2017 survey titled "What People Want," conducted by recruiting firm Hays US, found that more than half of those who were still working in construction said they were unhappy in their jobs. More than 80 percent said they would consider leaving. But money, it turns out, is not the primary issue.

In the same survey, Hays found that more than 70 percent of employees said they'd take a pay cut for the "ideal" job. An article on the Hays site summarizing the report has a headline that merits framing and hanging in the room where candidates are interviewed: "US workers willing to compromise on salary for the right benefits, company culture, and career growth opportunities."

Companies are having to recruit, replace, and train about half of their younger workers, every year!

Turnover eats away at productivity, undermines good customer service, hampers quality control, inhibits opportunity, and erodes profitability. Tackling it should be a top priority. How to go about that is a challenge. The rewards come slowly but are well worth the investment.

My Hiring Epiphany

My epiphany about hiring began as a result of a project that didn't fit our company profile but that we took anyway because we needed the work. The job site was a condo complex that had been the subject of a lawsuit over faulty construction. The decks were rotting out long before they should have been because the original builder had cut corners.

It was a time and materials job on which we had about fifteen people working. Because of the shortage of skilled help, we were essentially hiring warm bodies. Predictably, a high percentage didn't work out so we were constantly having to find new candidates. This hiring–firing–hiring cycle sucked the energy out of the whole company. We learned a lot about what not to do.

Years later, at a Remodelers Advantage Summit in Las Vegas, I had a chance to hear a talk by a key executive with Zappos, the online shoe company that in just a few years had become a phenomenal success. Jon Wolske had played a central role in creating an environment that was so attractive that the company was ranked among *Fortune's* Top 100 Companies to Work For numerous times.

His mantra is culture, a word that is hard to define but that shares characteristics with the concept of family or community—inclusion, shared effort for shared benefit, and a devotion to great service to coworkers as well as to customers. I was struck by how his description of Zappos's onboarding process differs from what happens at the typical remodeling company, where a new hire spends maybe a day or two filling out forms and figuring out the wheres, whats, whos, and whens. Then they're thrown into the project that's most behind schedule.

According to Wolske, at Zappos every new hire—even the folks in the executive suite—go through a month of education and indoctrination into the Zappos culture. As part of the process, new hires put in a few days working at each of the essential positions in the company. A new customer service rep will spend some time in the shipping department and a new comptroller will spend time working a phone in the call center.

Among other benefits, a month of this baptism encourages some unsuitable candidates to self-select themselves out. It gives Zappos a chance to get to know their new hires before they put them in the harness. There's time to make last-minute switches in the lineup. Those who complete the orientation have walked a mile in everyone else's shoes, creating a sense of shared purpose and mission across the company that manifests itself in superior service and robust sales.

But you're not Zappos. No remodeling firm can afford to spend a month orienting a new lead carpenter or production manager, but the principle is the same—hire methodically. The first step is figuring out where to find the best candidates.

CHAPTER 7

Hunting For Help

T HE IDEAL CANDIDATES for positions in your firm are so good they already have a job. Thus they are less likely to see, let alone respond to, a want ad you might place. You have to do more than sit back and wait for them to show up. This is where networking can really pay off.

Your Competitors

Although at first it can sound to owners I work with as counterintuitive, the competition can be a great resource. A In 2014, Zeke Adkins, cofounder of Luggage Forward, wrote in *Entrepreneur Magazine* about his experience after the company's board of directors encouraged him to get to know his competition.

The competition can be a great resource.

"At first we were unsure of the benefits but we dutifully set out to get to know everyone in our industry. Without exception, our calls and emails were well received," Adkins reported, leading to relationships with about a dozen companies. "We were able to work together to determine the best way to satisfy customers. It was a win-win for everyone around."

Look around your market. Which companies have the best reputations, the longest track records, the highest customer satisfaction scores, are growing in spite of premium pricing? Aren't you curious how they got started, and how they became so successful?

Once you've identified a couple, gather your courage and reach out with an email or letter inviting the owner out for coffee or a meal. There are a lot of good reasons to get to know others in your field, but surprisingly few remodeling companies do it. What to say? Do some research on their recent projects and any news stories they may have been mentioned in. Then try a bit of honest flattery.

Dear Joe,

I was driving down Main Street the other day and noticed that you've finished the Victorian remodel at the corner of State Street. It looks great and you must be proud. Knowing how complex a project like that is, and others I've seen that were done by your firm, I've come to admire your good reputation and commitment to quality work.

Because we seem to share similar values, I thought it might be interesting to meet, talk shop, and possibly explore how we might be helpful to each other. For example, we recently hired a production manager and there were some great candidates we had to turn down who might have been a good fit for a firm such as yours.

Leave the setting open ended. Some competitors will ignore your invitation, but my experience has been that most remodeling company owners are receptive and often eager to chat with a fellow traveler. Some will be cautious and choose the quick cup of coffee. Others will welcome the chance to spend a couple of hours over a great meal (your treat), swapping war stories and trading professional gossip. It's what lawyers and medical professionals do all the time.

When you do find a competitor who agrees to meet, at some point in the conversation you'll want to ask, "So, Joe, how can I help you?" In my experience, chances are good your guest will be a bit surprised and even flustered. It's an unexpected question coming from a peer.

What follows may be a discussion about the sorts of clients that the company does best with, or—like you—it may be staff related: "Boy, I'd sure like to find an estimator I can trust!" By the time you pay the bill, you may have an ally who just might know of a great candidate but couldn't hire the person because the position was already filled. Get to know enough of your competitors and you may find they're open to meeting periodically as an informal trade association.

Other Resources

Your suppliers can also be sources for leads to good job candidates. They are serving your competitors and, in addition to having unique insights into your market, they may also know about good employees at other firms that are dissatisfied and thinking about making a move. Talk to your subcontractors' best craftspeople, the folks who are actually doing the work as opposed to the salespeople. They know the best lead carpenters. So do architects. When you need one, you may be able to recruit one who has already been vetted and has a good reputation.

Talk with local home builders who may have retreated to remodeling during a downturn but are back at their principal businesses of new home construction. Some of them may have employees who turned out to be more adept at remodeling and may now be struggling.

Tech schools and community colleges often have degree and continuing education programs in construction management. Talk to the teachers and professors about any outstanding students they may have identified.

Tips For Want Ads

When you're unable to find candidates from within your circle of influence—professional, personal, community—you'll do what your competitors are doing: advertising. In the ads you write, go beyond describing the basics of the position. The top applicants will be those who have a reason to think your company might be a great place to work with a future—better than the other guys. As the Hays US survey found, people are looking for more than just a job. They want to feel good about where they work and who they work with.

Here is an example of a want ad that the employer must have hoped would weed out all the people who weren't absolutely perfect specimens so as to end up with the ideal hire on a silver platter. I doubt it worked.

Skilled superintendent/tradesman sought. Must possess journeyman-level ability in carpentry, drywall, paint, ceramic tile. Paperwork and customer service skills are critical components of this position. Work includes nights and weekends as customer schedule dictates and includes some travel within a two-state market. Exceptional opportunity for long-term employment with competitive pay, benefits, and travel allowances. We are an equal opportunity employer with a strong supportive team. Reference/background check and drug testing are part of employment screening. Respond with description of skills and contact information.

That's a rather grim description of a job, with a set of requirements few candidates would be able to meet. This company's message was: Don't even bother applying unless:

- You're multi-skilled.
- You have no private life to interfere with those nights, weekends, and travel.
- You don't mind staying up late writing reports.
- You have a background as pure as driven snow
- You have the personal habits of a monk.

Maybe the company was more realistic than the ad makes it sound. Maybe it was even a great place to work. But most people would be so turned off they wouldn't take the time to find out.

For contrast, here's another ad that has a lot of heart, speaks to possibilities, appeals to aspirations, and even tells a story.

Carpenter position available! ABC Builders is a small residential remodeling company with an excellent track record of quality work and professionalism and over seven years in business. We are looking for a carpenter to assist in the building and possible leadership of a wide range of projects, including: additions, interior remodeling, doors and windows. Our current carpenter is moving out of state, opening up an opportunity for a hard-working individual with a minimum of three years in the field or tech school experience in carpentry. Experience in other fields of construction is a bonus. Pay based on experience. Jobs are generally located within our suburban metro area. Please email me with your contact information, and I will call for a brief phone interview within a day.

Although the requirements for this job are less demanding than the first example, the ad has the warm and fuzzy feel that is more likely to snag the attention of typically busy, anxious job hunters. This company is telling prospects:

- We're proud of our work and our reputation.
- We're in it for the long haul.
- We're flexible on experience.

- We need a carpenter to replace someone who we would have kept on, not someone who was fired or quit.
- Your commutes will be reasonable.
- You don't need a resume to get your foot in the door.
- You will be dealing with the boss.
- And, we respect your time and dignity—we won't keep you guessing.

In addition to writing your ad to appeal directly to job candidates, consider trying ads with headlines that might catch the eye of a spouse helping with the search. A couple of headlines from Craigslist ads:

"Remodeling Foreman: Weekends and Holidays Off!!"

"Remodeling Sales: A 2018 Top-Ranked Workplace!"

CHAPTER 8

Hire Slow, Fire Fast

THE HIRING PROCESS THAT WORKED well for our company—which we learned the hard way—begins with having someone in the office call those who answered the ad as opposed to someone in production who might be so focused on skills they'd miss some warning signs. We made a list of things that drove us crazy about the people who had held the position before and turned those aggravations into questions that helped weed out people with similar traits or behaviors.

Intake And Interview Tips

Train your intaker to ask open-ended questions that cannot be answered by "yes" or "no." Terry Gross, the host of the popular NPR interview program *Fresh Air*, has said she finds the best icebreaker is simply, "Tell me a little about yourself." Encourage follow-up questions. Avoid the natural instinct to comment or interrupt. An awkward silence now and then allows people time to think before speaking—a good quality in a potential hire.

The goal of this stage is to gather an impression as opposed to just facts. Based on how the initial phone interview goes, the next step is to whittle the list down and ask the "keepers" to come in and fill out an application. When they do, pay attention! Don't just stick them in a cubicle and forget about them. You'll learn a lot about habits, priorities, and attitudes by taking note of a few key behaviors.

Did they show up at the appointed hour? Did your applicant come prepared with a pen or pencil and notepad? Did they have questions about the position? We used a short application form—several pages asking for just the basics—that we knew could be completed in less than fifteen minutes. A candidate who was still fussing with it after a half hour was considered unlikely to be a good fit.

When interviewing those applicants who make the cut, you should allow for nervousness. Some people who interview poorly can make great employees.

In our company, instead of taking people's word about their skills, we developed simple tests that were relevant to what they'd actually be doing. For example, we had them write a message to a client about a technical or financial issue. To make it even more relevant, we gave applicants only ten minutes to do it, just as much time as they'd have in a real situation. We learned a lot about how well people communicated, how they solved problems, and how they performed under pressure.

Avoid discussing money until the end of the interview, once you have a clear idea of what skill level—and thus what value—they will bring to your operations and profitability and you feel confident the candidate is someone you'd want to hire. Rather than talking about what you are prepared to pay, ask candidates what they are looking to earn. It's not a trick question. If a person's expectations are unrealistic, you want to know about that before offering them a job that will fail to meet their needs from day one.

If a person's expectations are more modest than you've budgeted, you can make a new hire feel special by offering them a higher rate of pay, sending the message, "Hey, we really want you on our team and we're willing to pay to make it happen." Or you could decide to hire them at the rate they're seeking and preserve for later the option for a quick raise if they seem to be working out.

Hire, Then Cultivate

As we refined our hiring process, Nina and I came to realize that before actually making an offer, no matter how perfect the person seemed to us, we needed to have buy in from the production staff. It was a gesture of respect at first, but we discovered that our crew became more invested in the new hire's success. We were building culture!

The goal of methodical hiring is to reduce the number of people who turn out to be duds two or three weeks in. Hiring is often viewed by owners and managers as a necessary nuisance. Once they've made the decision, they may be so worn out that they'll do just about anything to justify keeping that person on to avoid having to go through the whole process again. They will often tell themselves that the new hire is "probably going to get better"—until they've

THE REMODELING LIFE ~ Paul L. Winans

been on the team so long it's hard to let them go without a compelling reason. Remember, you're running a business, not a charity.

One of the more effective changes we made was to have the person who would be managing a new hire conduct an initial chat in a neutral location outside the office—a coffee shop for example, or even just the tailgate of a pickup truck. That conversation goes something like this:

"I'll be asking you two questions once a week for the next six weeks. Every time we meet, you'll give me your answers. Then I'll answer them from my perspective. The first question will be, From your perspective, what's been going really well with your work at our company?

Remember, you're running a business, not a charity.

"Your answer needs to be more than 'I feel comfortable.' Give me an example of when you felt most comfortable, what you were doing, who you were doing it with, what happened."

What you're looking for from your new hire is along the lines of, "Something wasn't going as well as I wanted. Bill coached me and I got an insight about how to handle this craft problem. Bill made me feel like I'm part of the team." That's real information. So too are shrugged shoulders and vague comments—"Everybody seems real nice"—which tells you this person doesn't pay attention to details.

The second question you'll be asking each week is, "What could be going better with your work at our company?" It's important to let new hires understand they won't be penalized for being up front about their struggles. This process can help alert you to project problems that might otherwise go unnoticed until the fix has become complex and expensive.

If your employee comes back with an example of a situation where they felt stressed, made a mistake, had to be corrected, or should have been better prepared, that's a good sign. If what you get instead are excuses, complaints about the behavior of coworkers or clients, or some other off point reply, you have a problem that ought to be nipped in the bud.

Once the new hire has given the weekly answers, the manager cites an example of something the employee did well and some aspect where improvement is needed. Then close the interaction with: "Let's agree that you're going to focus on getting better at this one thing by the time we meet again a week from now." By the sixth week, you should have already fired a person who's clearly struggling, and you'll have some expectation that the person who is still there has become a valued team member.

Some Firing Tips

As I stressed earlier, you want to slow down the process of hiring and be decisive about the process of firing. Done well and consistently, you'll find you need to do less of either. Firing is stressful, but more often than not the rest of your people will breathe a collective sigh and even thank you.

The lesson: It's harder to get great performances from good employees when you hang on to those who aren't good employees. Failure to act sends a negative message. Cutting your losses is a sign of respect for the rest of the team.

Letting an underperforming or unsuitable employee go is also an opportunity to build loyalty. As soon as possible after the person is gone, hold a brief staff meeting to make it official. Explain that it was a decision made for the good of the business, the working conditions of everyone else, and the benefit of the clients. Remind them that they continue to be employed because they are part of the solution and that you are gratified to be working with a great crew.

Open the discussion for brief comments and questions. Encourage everyone in attendance to have their say, or articulate their feelings. It's your job to moderate the discussion to keep it short and steer it away from personal attacks or judgmental remarks. Doing so will give everyone an increased sense of shared purpose and commitment. You will have turned a challenging moment into a win. You'll also have relieved yourself of having to repeatedly answer the question, "So, what really happened with Joe?"

For more reading on this, I found a lot of great, detailed ideas in *Hiring Smart!: How To Predict Winners and Losers in the Incredibly Expensive People-Reading Game* by Pierre Mornell, a psychiatrist and recruiting consultant. It's the most useful book I've read on the subject.

CHAPTER 9

Ideal Hires

N O MATTER HOW WELL-RUN your company may
be, no matter how terrific your customer service, no
matter how superior the quality of your work, it's important
to remember that this is a people business. While you're
in the office keeping the trains running on time, your lead
carpenters and production managers are out there inter-
acting with customers. Whether a job is successful and a
customer is satisfied can depend on factors that have nothing
to do with the work itself and everything to do with the
personalities of the people you hire.

Why Social Skills Matter

This was a lesson learned when we hired a lead carpenter
with decent credentials and assigned him to run a project
for a customer we'd had for many years who was delight-
ful to work with. We had successfully completed several
projects for her and she had become one of our biggest fans.
For years she had worked with another fellow on our team
and we'd heard no complaints.

Although the new guy was a bit reticent during the
interview process and very private about his personal life,

he seemed to be more than competent and experienced and that was what we needed at the time. Soon after he was assigned to our star client, I got a call from her.

"He never tells me what's going on," she said. "I never know what's about to happen or what's getting done. He never starts a conversation with me. I have to ask things and this is so different from the way it worked before."

There was nothing wrong with the work and it was getting done on time and budget. But the person she had been working with before was more engaging. He and our client had bonded over the years, and in a sense he had become a principal reason she kept using us. The new guy was more awkward with people than I realized. He avoided company functions, and when he couldn't he didn't have much to say.

The client was important to us, practically a member of the team after all that time, so in the middle of this latest project we swapped the new guy out and brought the other one back. As our operation was all client centered and we expected our leads and managers to be able to manage relationships with trade contractors and vendors as well, we eventually had to let the new fellow go.

Matching Personalities With Jobs

After that experience, we began to think about personality styles when hiring. Up until then we hired people who presented well, were easy conversationalists, and seemed to be sociable. But it turns out that someone who likes to chat may be one of those people who has trouble getting things done on time or on budget. We once hired a lead carpenter who had a great personality and a natural smile. He loved to talk. But after carefully figuring out the correct cut on a special order beam that was huge and expensive, he was so distracted by chatting with his workmates that he cut it too short.

I began to research how we could assess someone's fitness for a position by asking the right questions before we offered them the job. No two candidates are ever alike, but there has been a great deal of interesting work done on personality or behavior types that some companies have found useful in the quest for the ideal lead carpenter, production manager, estimator, or office manager.

The most important thing I've learned about business is how important it is to keep learning about yourself.

DiSC is the acronym for one of the most popular psychological assessment tools used by companies today. I have employed it from time to time as a prompt to help consulting clients think about matching personality types with job requirements when recruiting and hiring. DiSC is designed to organize personality types into four basic behavioral styles. It was popularized in 1928 by William Marston, a Harvard—educated psychologist.

DiSC stands for Dominance, Influence, Steadiness,

and Conscientiousness. Without getting into the weeds of Marston's approach, here are some basic descriptor words and inclinations associated with each.

D: Dominant, decisive, driver, determined: faster paced, results oriented

I: Influencer, inspirer, impulsive: faster paced, people oriented

S: Steady, supportive, secretive: slower paced, people oriented

C: Controlling, conscientious, cautious: slower paced, results oriented

Human resource consultants and others provide versions of DiSC assessment "tests" that we researched. There are free ones you can take online in about fifteen minutes and that, if nothing else, will give you food for thought and might give you insights into your management style. From time to time we used these tools in our business and found them helpful in educating ourselves about different character types and in identifying people who might be the best fit for each position.

Understanding Your Own Personality

The most important thing I've learned about business is how important it is to keep learning about yourself, testing your strengths and managing your vulnerabilities. Using these tools, I came to understand that I'm so results and action oriented that I can become impatient with people and a bit quick to act. So we adjusted. As I describe in Chapter Four, the result was my banishment from solo visits to job sites and I learned to balance my critiques with compliments.

We asked everyone in the company to take the DiSC survey and read their assessment, paying particular attention to their communication habits. Then each was asked to share with the rest of the company three things that caused them to tune out and three things that tended to keep them engaged.

For example, Nina is more methodical than I am. She takes time to process things before making a decision or acting. So I might go into her office all wound up: "I've got this problem. We need to respond quickly. What do you think of my solution? We don't have time to think it over!" Nina would immediately shut down, just waiting for me to leave so she could think it over.

After the DiSC exercise, I adjusted my approach, writing down what I needed help with and my proposed solution. That slowed me down and made my approach less off-putting. I would give it to Nina, asking her, "Could you review this? Would it be okay if I came back in ten minutes to talk about what we should do?" This process helped improve the company's productivity and made working with everyone else less stressful.

We learned that the ideal lead carpenter is someone who can take direction from others—like a production manager—as opposed to being a take-charge person. The ideal lead carpenter would additionally score high for following rules—also a good thing as long as it didn't lead to getting bogged down trying to solve inconsequential problems.

You want clients to feel that the lead carpenter is paying attention to and caring about them, so the ideal candidate would tend to place the needs of others first as a way of getting approval—a good thing so long as it didn't lead to doing extra work above and beyond the budget. We learned to avoid lead carpenter candidates who tended to be gregarious and thus might be prone to making mistakes due to being distracted.

We identified the ideal production manager as someone who is naturally assertive and in charge but is flexible enough to cope with all manner of hassles, from personnel to balky suppliers to cranky clients, without overstepping an invisible line between being decisive and dictatorial. The ideal production manager is able to sell a vision to other members of the team, good at negotiating change orders, good at holding vendors to their commitments and prices, and good at coaching others. You want a good problem solver in a role where just about everything begs for a solution.

We profiled the ideal office manager as someone who is comfortable taking direction but also is comfortable speaking their mind without letting issues smolder. This position works closely with a variety of personalities, so the ideal candidate would be naturally sociable while being able to think and act responsibly without waiting for approval, would help others stay on track and meet deadlines in a supportive and open way, would be the "mother hen" to clients and everyone on your team, and would represent the company to others professionally and respectfully.

This is such a key position that it's wise to be fussy. Be prepared to fail the first time out. If your hire turns out to be a dud who's distracting you from your responsibilities, avoid hanging on in hopes of improvement. Put yourself out of your misery, let the person go, deal with the turmoil, and try again.

Psychological profiling is not the be-all and end-all of hiring. I've referred to it mainly to provoke you into thinking about the behaviors and attitudes that make someone a better fit than another. You can decide that profiles are mumbo jumbo but still get some benefits and insights out of knowing what they are and how they are interpreted.

Additional resources we found useful include: *I'm Stuck, You're Stuck: Break Through to Better Work Relationships and Results by Discovering Your DiSC Behavioral Style* by Tom Ritchey with Alan Axelrod, and *The Essential Enneagram: The Definitive Personality Test and Self-Discovery Guide* by David Daniels and Virginia Price.

CHAPTER 10

Assume Nothing

H IRING IS NEVER a set-it-and-forget-it function. That is, however, a common default in many businesses and the cost can be steep, especially when you allow your emotions to cloud your business judgment.

Remodeling Your Office

A consulting client I once worked with had a bookkeeper who, when we met, I had an instinct about—a doubt I couldn't quite describe, but a strong one. She was pleasant and personable but I had a feeling she was in over her head. She took a long time providing answers for my questions, and the answers were a bit convoluted. When I mentioned this to the owner, he explained that this person had experienced a lot of tragedy and hardship in her life and he'd kept her on because she needed the income. She had become a project instead of a solution.

I suggested he invest in an outside accounting professional to teach her how to keep proper books. He did, and when the accountant got down to looking over the company's records in detail, it was clear something was seriously wrong. The accountant produced a thirty-page report of improper entries and errors, including a discrepancy between the amount of cash on hand showing in the books and actual cash in the bank. The owner had to ask the bank to freeze his accounts until the mess could be sorted out. And he had to find a new bookkeeper.

Although Nina was primarily responsible for our books, I wanted to be able to decipher those numbers on my own, so I took some accounting classes at the local community college. It's a small investment that can pay big dividends. Your financial records tell a story and sometimes it's not the same story you're telling yourself. Gross revenue may be up and you feel like you're making progress, but what if your expenses are rising faster? It's the same principle as the one that drives Zappos—you don't have to be able to do every job in the company, but you should know how every job in the company is supposed to be done.

Beware The Office Spouse

A phenomenon I've noticed in my consulting practice is that many companies have a person I've come to call the Office Spouse—an employee who isn't a spouse but acts like it, even to the point of bullying the boss. This is usually a longtime trusted employee who has been given—or has had conceded to them—too much authority without accountability. The Office Spouse enjoys taking care of the things the owner likes least. In time, the owner loses track of just what this employee does or how it gets done.

Like the main characters in the Neil Simon play *The Odd*

Couple, it's not uncommon for this arrangement to one day just blow up. The owner gets tired of being browbeaten by the Spouse. Or the owner discovers that the Spouse isn't as competent as he or she appeared. Or, worse, the Spouse has been embezzling.

If you think it couldn't happen to you, or that someone you trust would never betray you, a couple of statistics might give you pause. A 2016 study on embezzlement by Hiscox, a global specialist insurer, found that small and midsize firms accounted for two out of every three embezzlement cases, with median losses per case of nearly $300,000. In cases where stealing went undiscovered for five or more years, the average loss was $2.2 million, and those which went on for a decade or more resulted in average losses of $5.4 million.

Your financial records tell a story and sometimes it's not the same story you're telling yourself.

Hiscox reported that the profile of an embezzler is often a valued employee, someone who tends to be extra curious about how the company works and who is eager to be the go-to person for problem solving. They're diligent and ambitious, coming to work early and leaving late and passing up opportunities for vacations, which is when a lot of cases are discovered.

There's such a thing as a good Office Spouse, and there's nothing wrong with investing a staffer with your trust. But if you start to feel that someone you trust is irreplaceable, think again. They may seem indispensable, but the only person who cannot be replaced is you. Go ahead and trust—but verify. Take the time to periodically have a key person walk you through their tasks. Assume nothing. Ask questions. Do this a few times a year and you'll be less likely to wake up one day to a crisis and a messy "divorce."

Basic protections include buying insurance (your insurer will do the appropriate background check), not giving an administrative employee the right to sign checks, and having statements mailed to your home.

Embezzling is more common than we care to believe, especially because many cases are never pursued. Recovery is more often than not unlikely. It's embarrassing for your clients, vendors, and other employees to know that you failed to detect what was happening right under your nose. And frequently the miscreant otherwise did a good job or was considered a friend whom you are reluctant to punish beyond firing.

If something feels off about an employee in a key position, chances are it won't get better the longer the person works for you. People who seem otherwise caring, thoughtful, and loyal—even relatives—are capable, under the right circumstances, of making some terrible choices.

CHAPTER 11

Connecting The Dots

ONE OF THE CHALLENGES of putting together a compendium of advice for owners of remodeling companies is that the majority of you did not set out to found a remodeling company. You likely launched your professional life with a toolbox, a pickup, and a lunch pail. The company grew up around you the way grapevines take over a pergola, season by season. You hired a helper. You had to buy a second truck. You rented a garage for a workshop. And so on. One day you suddenly realized you had a company. This is why many remodelers need help with understand how to build and sustain a company culture, create a mission statement and values, and encourage team building.

What Culture?

The concept of culture—defining it and building on it—leaves many remodelers scratching their heads. Mission statement? "We do quality work" doesn't cut it. Core values? "Honest work for an honest buck" is not a value nor does it tell anyone about YOUR company. In Part Three, you will find some thoughts and suggestions about mission statements if you don't have one, or don't like the one you have.

For now, I'm focusing on how to indoctrinate new hires in such a way that they feel valued and lucky to be working for you. As part of the onboarding process, share your backstory. Why were you crazy enough to start a business? What were you thinking when you worked for your bosses? What are some pivotal moments in your work life? By sharing information like this with your employees, they will have an opportunity to learn how you think and what you expect of them.

To do this, it may help to sit down and make some notes about yourself, your motivations, some turning points in the company's history, and what you think makes your company a great place to work. Ask yourself some basic questions, such as:

What makes your company different from other remodeling companies?

What are the attributes that make someone a good employee for your company?

What do you want clients to think and feel when they interact with an employee of your company?

What behavior is unacceptable to the company?

As part of this process, you could tell stories about how other employees have contributed to making the company what it is and their a role in creating your mission statement and establishing your core values. Taking the time to address these aspirational ideas with a new hire will make it more likely that they'll stop and think before doing something that could damage the reputation of the company. In telling the company story to a new hire you are making them part of the story—and thus, the team—from day one.

Making Sure Everyone Gets It

Rather than just handing a new hire an envelope full of paper to take home, the office manager should sit down with that person and go over documents such as the employee manual. The new employee is likely to be overwhelmed by so much information all at once. Allow enough time that they can feel comfortable asking questions and you will feel confident that they are "getting it."

You can learn a lot about someone by sharing a meal. You and another employee could take the new person out for lunch on the first day. Observe how they conduct themselves. Are they easy conversationalists or does it take work to engage them? What questions do they ask? The insights that come from this informal social situation can help when matching coworkers up on a job and can suggest areas to work on or look out for with a new employee.

In telling the company story to a new hire you are making them part of the story—and thus, the team—from day one.

Assign your new hire a training partner, an experienced coworker they can work side by side with for a few days at least, and a full week if possible. As described in Chapter 8, there should be a feedback session during which the partner or a supervisor discusses what went well and where some work is needed. This interaction wraps up with the employee and the partner/manager agreeing about one thing the employee should focus on improving over the coming week. When they meet again, the two of them will review what progress has been made.

When the occasion arises, the training partner should introduce the new employee to clients, observe how they interact with them, and then coach them as necessary.

Team-Building Tips

One way for a new hire to feel more engaged and comfortable is by briefly sharing personal histories with the team during weekly meetings. This idea was borrowed from one of the many books I read over the years—*The Five Dysfunctions of a Team* by management consultant Patrick Lencioni. I found it particularly useful. Lencioni suggests asking each person to give five quick facts about themselves: Hometown, number of siblings, childhood hobbies or interests, the biggest challenge they faced growing up, and their first job.

The first time we did this, we learned that many of our people had started working in their early teens and thus had learned good work habits right from the start. Sharing helped connect the dots among and between employees.

Over the years, I learned that someone who looks great on day one may not look so good a month or two later. We adopted a policy of hiring people with a probationary period of ninety days, enough time to establish whether they were keepers. If someone failed to make the cut, we reviewed the hiring process to try to figure out how to avoid making the same mistake in the future.

When we first started our company, we did not have a mission statement, a written set of core values, or an employee manual. These documents are to companies what enology, the science of winemaking, is to a vineyard. It takes time and the right conditions to develop them. Until you do, make detailed notes during your weekly meetings with employees. When you start writing down the same thoughts, you're probably ready to boil it all down into an employee manual. You may also have the fodder you need for mission and core value statements.

Another approach is to pick a thought-provoking book and have everyone read it, a chapter or a few pages a week. One of the books we used was Stephen Covey's *The 7 Habits of Highly Effective People.* He suggests techniques to get you and your team thinking. Buy copies of the book for everyone and schedule meetings every couple of weeks to talk about what they were assigned to read. Keep the selections short. Nobody likes homework! Schedule the meeting at the end of the day, provide snacks, and, of course, pay your employees for that time.

As the leader of this book club, remember to be a facilitator as opposed to an instructor. Ask questions about how the book might be affecting the choices people have made. It may take forever to get through the book, but speed is not the goal. The book is a prompt for discussions that will undoubtedly lead to positive change as people reflect on what they are reading and what was discussed. We found that new, positive behaviors began to emerge without people being conscious of it happening.

When the book is finished, invite your fellow readers to contribute their thoughts about a mission statement: "Based on what we read and based on your experiences working here, what do you think our mission statement should be?" Let them know that you are taking input from them only for consideration, that the final version will be your call. Before the next meeting, distribute your draft and get feedback. Make the final changes and then print it. The same process works for developing core values.

At the end of all this, you will have remodeled your staff. You and your people will be more in sync and more of a team. You will have created your unique culture, which will help you be more efficient at recruiting and retaining the best people.

None of this is quite as simple and straightforward in practice as it sounds in theory. You will no doubt have moments when you're frustrated, irritated, and exasperated. You are by definition an entrepreneur. Entrepreneurs get their greatest satisfaction from building a business, solving problems, overcoming challenges, and all the demands that doing so entails.

When you do get steamed or impatient with your employees, try to remember that they have other interests that give them fulfillment. While you live to work, your people work to live. Always keep that in mind.

PART III

Remodel Your Business

CHAPTER 12

Consult For Yourself

I
T'S THE RARE FOUNDER of a remodeling company whose career began with the dream of owning and running such a complex enterprise. When you feel overwhelmed by it all, you may ask yourself, as I sometimes did: How did I get here? What was I thinking?

Thinking has little to do with it. For many owners, it feels as if one day they were young and full of spirit, swinging a hammer and hefting bags of cement, and the next they were having to learn how to woo prospects, produce accurate estimates, and close sales; how to hire, train, manage, pay, and fire people; how to source and price materials; how to plow through piles of paperwork; how to juggle cash flow through lean spells; and, through it all, how to stay sane and healthy.

If you're like many of the people I work with, every day is a challenge just to keep up. It's like standing, bat in hand, in a practice cage facing a rapid-fire pitching machine with an unlimited supply of baseballs. There's no time to think. You have to just keep swatting. The occasional pause—a day when everything clicks, the news is good, the sun is shining—is so rare it triggers more anxiety than a day of dawn-to-dusk crises.

If you've read Part One, you've thought about how to remodel yourself in relation to your business. If you've read Part Two, you've thought about how you recruit, train, develop, and manage the people you depend on to keep it going. The next step is to remodel how you organize and manage your business. How can you develop, refine, and institutionalize procedures that redistribute some of the responsibilities that distract you from the big picture? How can you run your business so that it doesn't run you?

This is the point when I'm often asked to come in, when owners and managers are stuck in a dysfunctional pattern, overwhelmed, and in need of a fresh set of eyes. A professional consultant can provide objective, practical feedback and insights—moments of revelation and confirmation. Whatever challenge you're grappling with right now, I've seen and dissected it dozens of times.

Tune Your Attitude

You don't have to wait until there's a crisis to summon the cavalry. You can get started by learning to be your own consultant. It's not a cinch, it has many moving parts, and it takes time. But it can be done as long as you're prepared to close your mouth and open your ears—not always natural when you're the boss of your own business. Anything that displeases or frustrates you can at times feel like a personal affront, a bruise to the ego.

It was hard for me, as I describe in Chapter 4. I had a filter on my vision that only let me see the things that needed fixing or improving. All the crew heard from me was grumbling. When our production manager began to chaperone me to sites and I was allowed to mention to the crew only the things I was happy about, it was frustrating at first. I'm by nature a go-to person—a problem solver, a decider. Having the answers appealed to my sense of self. I was the person in the batting cage, swatting away. That's what a boss does, right?

Yes, but ... there are so many flaws with that approach. It wears you down and saps your creativity. It robs you of time for reflection, long-term planning, vacations. It makes you a choke point in the decision-making process. It stifles your employees' creativity, discourages them from thinking for themselves, and, worse, makes them reticent to come to you with concerns you should know about and ideas you could use.

The more essential you are to the operation of your business, the less essential your team members perceive themselves. Feeling less trusted, they grow less loyal and become more likely to look elsewhere for job satisfaction. That leads to turnover, that huge but hard-to-define expense that could deserve its own line in your budget.

Most recently, during the tight labor market of 2017 and 2018, attracting and retaining key people became a major headache in the construction and home building industries. Among builders surveyed in early 2019 by the National

Association of Home Builders, when asked about problems they recently had confronted or expected to confront, 80 percent named labor availability as a major problem.

Meanwhile, the supply of eager young workers is dwindling. Millennials are less attracted to the building trades than earlier generations. In a hypergrowth market like Colorado, an organization called Colorado Homebuilding Academy has been experimenting with eight-week boot-camps where young people can learn basic construction skills that prepare them for entry-level jobs.

The more essential you are to the operation of your business, the less essential your team members perceive themselves.

As your own consultant, instead of just enduring the churn, consider what you can do to slow it down by making sure your firm is more than a way station on someone's else's journey. You want to strive to be the employer of choice. You do that by developing, encouraging, and transforming your key people from followers of orders to collaborators and even consultants, like the production manager who helped me make our job sites more rewarding places to work.

General Colin L. Powell, a highly decorated chairman of the Joint Chiefs of Staff and a former US Secretary of State, has written and spoken extensively about the elements of leadership. One particular insight of his rings true in any enterprise, military or otherwise: "The day soldiers stop bringing you their problems is the day you have stopped leading them. They have either lost confidence that you can help or concluded you do not care."

A similar bit of wisdom was offered by Calvin Coolidge, our thirtieth President: No one, he said, "has ever listened himself out of a job."

Listening, however, is not a passive tactic. Begin your business remodel by answering fewer questions and asking more. "What happened?" "How did it happen?" "What will be the result if we do nothing?" "What do you think is a good solution?" "What will implementing the solution cost in money and time?"

Your goal as owner is getting the business and seeing that the work is done, the bills are paid, and a profit is earned. The most important work you can do to get that result is helping people learn to think for themselves. Slow down and coach them to look beyond the immediate problem to see the big picture. Remind yourself and them that you all are in this endeavor together and that it is a journey, not a destination.

Investing in your relationships with your employees will make them more successful, and their success will drive yours.

CHAPTER 13

Facilitate, Don't Dominate

E VERYTHING I'VE LEARNED about business in general and the remodeling business in particular came to me the hard way. Looking back, my management style in the early years qualified me as difficult to work for—and sometimes worse.

I lectured instead of interviewing potential hires. I repeated instructions as if doing so made them clearer or increased the chances they would be followed. I tended to overreact, criticize, and catastrophize, and I generally operated under a dark cloud of anxiety that shadowed me from crisis to crisis. I drove myself and others crazy.

I knew something had to change, but the insight was slow in developing and progress came in fits and starts. The single most valuable experience I had before we sold our company was the opportunity to participate in and ultimately to facilitate peer-to-peer gatherings for a Maryland–based consulting group, Remodelers Advantage. The firm specializes in helping small to midsized companies with everything from culture to processes.

Networking

We joined a peer group in 1994 and were members until we sold our business. In 2000, seven years before we sold, I began facilitating peer group meetings for Remodelers Advantage. Altogether I have been involved in peer group activities for more than twenty-five years.

It would never have occurred to me on my own, isolated within my industry and from competitors within my market, to sit down at a table with a group of other remodeling execs to share challenges and swap ideas. These peer groups are made up of owners and execs of noncompeting companies, removing the implied risk of revealing more to rivals than you'd like.

As I learned by facilitating others, there's a strong argument to be made for seeing your peers as potential advisors. Lawyers have bar associations, real estate agents routinely network, every state has a banking association—so why not remodelers? It took me awhile to figure out that some of the most helpful consultants were on my payroll or just across town.

During those years of facilitating the breakthroughs of others, I learned what I wished I'd known when I was starting out and began using it in our business.

Inspire, Don't Tell

To be your own consultant, your aim is to get others, especially employees, to feel safe opening up about how they feel and what they think. But you can't just sit people down and expect them to spontaneously confess all their frustrations, observations, and inspirations. The pressure of being in the spotlight makes many people feel vulnerable and they freeze up, or they say what they think you want to hear. Patience is required to help participants feel comfortable and safe raising their hands and contributing.

Ask Open-Ended Questions

Instead of questions that can be answered with a simple yes or no, ask questions that encourage thoughtful responses. A carpenter cuts a special-order beam too short and it can't be fixed. He already feels terrible, knowing it means an added expense to replace it and a disruption of the schedule. When you discuss it with him, you start out by asking: "So, tell me more. What was going on at the site at the time?" This leads to the 5 Whys, one of the most useful things I learned.

5 Whys

My patience was especially short with people who always offered excuses for why something went wrong, why they messed up, why they were late, and so on. A technique I learned about from another business owner helped me deal with the excuses while making my expectations clear and without getting too red in the face.

5 Whys is a technique for getting to the root cause of a specific problem. It's based on the premise that failure is a

process issue as opposed to a personnel problem. The genesis of 5 Whys is attributed to Sakichi Toyoda, the founder in 1926 of the company that became the industrial giant that is today's Toyota. Toyoda is said to be the father of Japan's industrial revolution.

Here are two examples of his 5 Whys, tweaked a bit to be more relevant in this context.

The problem: A project did not get done on schedule.

Excuse I: The electricians couldn't come when I needed them.

1. **Why not?**
   Answer: I was so busy getting other things done I didn't have time to coordinate with them.

2. **Why were you so busy?**
   Answer: It was a complex project with a lot to do and not enough time to do it all.

3. **Why wasn't there enough time?**
   Answer: I had a hard time keeping focused and organized.

4. **Why?**
   Answer: Every day I was falling farther behind and couldn't catch up.

5. **Why?**
   Answer: I didn't contact the subcontractors far enough ahead of time about when I would need them.

Excuse II: We won't be done on time because all the cabinet parts have not been delivered.

1. **Why not?**
   Answer: A scribe strip for the corner cabinet is missing.

2. **Why?**
   Answer: I don't know.

3. **Why not?**
   Answer: I had to go to the lumberyard.

4. **Why?**
   Answer: To exchange some hardware that was in a mislabeled box.

5. **Why?**
   Answer: I didn't examine the products when they were delivered so I only found out that something was wrong when I went to install them.

The 5 Whys conversation you have with a member of your team is an objective, results-oriented approach that helps that person identify the process glitch that caused the problem, so that they can better cope with similar issues in the future. The discussion becomes objective instead of personal.

Solve Instead of Blame

As a business owner, I was responsible for helping people take responsibility. It's hard to do when someone is in denial, defensive, or the only person in the room who thinks they are being misjudged.

Avoid personal pronouns. Instead of asking "How could you have …?", I learned to ask, "What could have been done differently?" Looking back at what cannot be changed is never as helpful as looking forward with a constructive and collaborative approach: "How can we change our procedures so this is less likely to happen again?"

Lead By Deed

At the beginning of each of the peer group meetings I facilitated, I announced that all phones were to be turned off. Then I took mine out of my pocket, shut it off with a subtle flourish, and put it away. Everyone got the message that I was serious without my having to say so.

Looking back at what cannot be changed is never as helpful as looking forward with a constructive and collaborative approach.

Meeting times should be etched in granite. For an 8 o'clock meeting, I made sure to be sitting down, paperwork and pad in front of me, my coffee at hand and having already made a quick trip to the bathroom, by 7:59:59. Time is the most precious commodity there is, yours especially. The first time you do this, the usual stragglers will be surprised. "You started without me?" Try this technique twice and no able-bodied employee will ever be late again.

CHAPTER 14

What's The Plan?

I F YOU'VE GOTTEN THIS FAR, you've probably had a brainstorm or two, have a clearer idea about the challenges your business is facing, and have some clues about how to tackle them. But putting what you've learned into practice can be daunting. The tendency is to grapple with the most immediate problems and crises as they pop up. You may reflexively think: I'm here. I know what's needed. I'll just deal with it myself.

Take A Step Back

It's time to step back, look at the big picture, and make a plan. To put it together, you'll need help. Unless or until you bring in a consultant, start by asking yourself a question that eludes many accidental entrepreneurs: Who can I get to help me do this? I often find that owners shortchange themselves by overlooking the hidden talent among their team members. Ideally, you will discover someone in your business who can be groomed to take on a role of coordinator—someone you can count on to help you herd the cats.

This person should enjoy creating order out of chaos—a results-oriented social person. In our business that was

Nina. In your company it may also be a spouse, or a partner, office manager, or someone you promote or hire to fill the role—coordinating, organizing, tracking, researching, and distilling all those ideas out of the ragged pile of notes, magazine clippings, brochures, and books.

Put your coordinator to work helping you sort through and prioritize the ideas, categorize them by department, and then pick the top two or three for each. Then you can set up a calendar of meetings to discuss and refine the ideas and out of it all make a plan to implement them.

In this process, solicit input from the rest of your team. That will encourage them to own it. Your coordinator should feel comfortable holding you, the owner, to account for completing your homework, attending meetings, and staying on schedule.

There are many good books and other resources to help you with the nuts and bolts of business planning and, most importantly, how to make sure the business is taking care of you and not the other way around. Two very different books on the subject are *Good to Great: Why Some Companies Make the Leap and Others Don't* by Jim Collins (the first of several books by this author) and *Run Your Business So It Doesn't Run You* by Linda Leigh Francis. Search Amazon's book listings and pick out a few on topics that interest you, or check out one of the books I've recommended here or in the resources list at the end. I've been an avid book reader most of my life, and the collective knowledge gleaned from the many business books I've read was essential in helping us to be able to retire early and sell the company as a going enterprise.

A popular book in recent years is *Traction: Get a Grip on Your Business* by Gino Wickman. The author offers a step-by-step process for remodeling your business to make it more likely you will be running it instead of the business running you. A number of people I consult with use Wickman's methodology in their business planning.

Hold Your Friends Close

As I discuss in Chapter 7, your competitors, vendors, and suppliers can be rich resources for remodeling your company. That sounded like a crazy idea when it was first proposed to me years ago, but I became a believer. We were invited to be part of an informal trade group put together by someone who had started his business at roughly the same time we did.

When we were asked to join, my first instinct was to decline. Talk to the enemy? Reveal our precious business secrets? Admit that we have challenges? Besides, in order to join I would have to give a live presentation about our work to the group. I had never done any speaking before and just the thought of doing so made me sweat.

On second look, I realized that the companies involved all seemed to be busy, craft oriented, and reputable. I didn't want to be left out. So I managed to survive giving my presentation and joined Artistic License, a guild of artisans and craftspeople working in the 1980s during a revival of interest in Victorians.

The members were all skilled professionals interested in historic restoration and newly reinterpreted period design. One person made silk screen reproductions of William Morris wallpapers. Others worked in stained glass restoration and tile painting. Our company was the group's general contractor. There were three different design people, two of them architects, and we worked with all three on amazing jobs we never would have gotten a chance to do otherwise.

There were multiple positive outcomes. Self-confidence. Inspiration. Alliances with other vendors. Cross-recommendations. And those Painted Lady Victorians were highly visible eye-poppers that enthusiasts would drive to see and photograph.

Defining Your Business

An important step in our planning was to define the company, articulate its purpose, identify its customers, and use all that to create our firm's culture. There are many guides and books on how to come up with things like mission statements, core values, and slogans. It's a stimulating and sometimes frustrating exercise. Why does your business exist? What is different about it? Why will potential clients want to work with your company instead of other companies?

Our mission statements and core values evolved as the company evolved and reflected a lot of input from our team members. As mentioned in Chapter 11, at a couple of points in the life of our company we all simultaneously read Covey's *7 Habits*. We bought everyone a copy, and every two weeks we were expected to have read the assigned chapters and be ready to discuss them. We met for an hour and had pizza delivered.

As facilitators, Nina and I focused the discussion on what effect those readings might be having on our employees' personal lives as well as their work. At the end of this exercise we revised our mission and values based on the feedback we'd gotten.

We routinely posted our mission and values on job sites where they could be seen by clients, professionals in other fields, and, as a reminder, ourselves. People noticed. One day a building inspector arrived on a site for a scheduled inspection and spotted the framed documents hanging on a stud near the job desk. He stopped short and stood there for the longest time reading them. Then he turned to the lead carpenter. "I've never seen a company put these up on a job site. That's just great." Without taking one more step, he signed the inspection paperwork and bid us a good day.

The mission statement that became our compass was straightforward: "Winans Construction consistently provides beautiful work with care on time and on budget. This creates satisfaction and loyalty with clients, staff, and outside providers." Our marketing motto was: "Beautiful Work With Care Since 1978."

Let's break that motto down. "Beautiful Work" didn't

mean "perfect." It meant that the lead carpenter had done what we sold to the clients and the clients loved the results. "With Care" meant that we were providing a positive experience for the client—something that would be more memorable to them than the actual remodel. "Since 1978" indicated longevity and meant that we had already made a lot of the mistakes needed to learn how to be a good remodeling company—which saved our clients the stress of working with someone who hadn't.

Plan your life first, and then plan your business to serve your life.

Choose your words in your mission statement and motto carefully, and make them all count.

Numbers Count

Nailing down the numbers that mattered most to us personally became the basis for our business planning over time. To get to those numbers, we set goals for the kinds and sizes of jobs we thought would be most likely to earn us the money we'd need to reach our personal goals.

One December we laid out one-, five-, ten-, and twenty-year goals for ourselves as a couple and individually. The simplest one was to see more movies. A big one was to travel abroad before our twenty-fifth wedding anniversary. We agreed we wanted to have our mortgage paid off by a specific date. I wrote that goal on a piece of paper that I kept in my wallet, so I could see it every time I reached for a credit card.

We beat those two big goals by a year each. We traveled abroad the year of our twenty-fourth anniversary and the mortgage was paid off a year ahead of our goal. The single most valuable lesson we learned is to plan your life first, and then plan your business to serve your life.

Here are some of the basic questions you can ask yourself to get a clearer sense of your relationship to your business and what you want it to do for you:

- How much annual salary do you expect/want the company to be paying you?

- How much net profit do you plan on the company generating so that, among other things, you will be able to give a bonus to yourself?

- What jobs/tasks do you want to be doing in your business?

- What jobs/tasks do you not want to be doing in your business?

- How many hours a week do you want to be working?

- How many weeks a year do you want to be working?

Simply thinking about the answers to these questions will help you remodel your business and plan so it will better serve you.

CHAPTER 15

Busy-ness

W<small>HEN</small> I <small>HEAR</small> the owner of a remodeling company
say, "I am so busy!" I wonder which busy they are
difference.

Frantic busy is the micromanager who is nervous or
unable to delegate, repeatedly checking the status of jobs,
interrupting the work that employees are supposed to be
doing, checking the mail (postal, email, messages), answering communications that could be handled by office staff,
and so on.

Frantic busy often means workflow is boom or bust. The
boom happens because the owner chases every lead, takes
jobs that are a poor fit, or has priced jobs to the bone, leaving
so little profit that the company has to take on more work
than it can handle just to keep cash flow from drying up.
New deposits pay old bills. Vendors and suppliers get tired
of waiting for checks and the firm has to find new sources
with liberal credit policies.

When the economy sags, bust comes early to the fran-
tically busy company because, among other reasons, it has
gotten a reputation for cutting corners, making design
mistakes, missing deadlines, or giving poor customer care.

"I'm so busy!" the owner tells anyone who'll listen. His friends and colleagues think he means things are going well when what he really means is, "I think I might be having a heart attack!"

Business busy means operating at a slower, steadier, more organized and measured pace. It means knowing what your company is best at, knowing what jobs to avoid, and learning from mistakes like one of mine many years ago that made me so frantic I decided I needed to get my head shrunk.

The Price Of Accommodation

It was a kitchen remodel for a couple Nina and I knew through the day care program our kids attended with their kids. We liked the couple a lot and I was looking forward to impressing them with our work.

They chose a line and style of cabinets that were at the high end, outside their budget. They entertained a lot and I thought the cabinets would make the finished result look so spectacular we'd get a referral or two. So I offered to let them order the cabinets direct from the manufacturer instead of through our company, saving them enough to stay within their budget. They thanked me, and I helped them place the order, made sure all the parts we'd need were in the order, and coordinated the delivery plan. No big deal. What could go wrong?

We had a delivery date and worked on a schedule to get the kitchen ready right on time so that the day the cabinets arrived we could unpack them and start the install. The big day arrived—no cabinets. More days passed and became weeks. Since I wasn't paying for the cabinets myself I had no leverage with the supplier. The job was stalled. My carefully laid plan for our workflow was upended and I was paying people to be on hold. The customer's kitchen was frozen in mid-project so they couldn't use it. And I became so frantic I felt like I could have had a heart attack.

I saw a therapist who warned me that it might take a few months to temper my frustration with things beyond my control. Afterward, I wrote down on a post-it note some tips and suggestions she made for getting my perspective back:

- Reorganize priorities.
- Fit in exercise.
- Do yoga/meditation to slow me down.
- Be positive.
- Nitpick less.
- This takes several months.

It's been a few decades since then and I'm still working on it! The post-it still is tacked on the wall in front of my desk, a little worn but still relevant.

The cabinets eventually arrived. The couple had been wonderfully patient and were delighted with the result. That was the last time I let a customer order cabinets from the manufacturer.

Learning To Pay Attention To Instinct

There were so many lessons that came out of that experience. If you are results oriented, you can't hand off control of any part of a project and be able to deliver those results the way you intend. I had not thought through the possible glitches and didn't have a process in place to talk it through with my team or anyone else who might have asked, "But, what if … ?"

I learned that straying from a process that works is risky, that results are what matter most, and that defining results is how you discover the process that works. The metric you use might be comparing projected to actual completion dates, budgeted to actual gross profit per project, and client satisfaction ratings. It almost does not matter how you measure it as long as the method is consistent with the results you want your company to achieve. It's a cliché but it's true: if you can't measure it, you can't manage it.

A book I found especially helpful is *Built to Sell: Creating a Business That Can Thrive Without You* by John Warrillow, a Toronto–based consultant. It had been recommended to me by several remodeling contractors I know and respect.

Warrillow's book is laid out as the story of a fictional business owner figuring out what he wants from his business—to be able to eventually sell it—and how his approach to business needs to change so he can achieve that. Alex, the business owner, has a series of conversations with a successful mentor, Ted, that help Alex move forward in his journey.

One of the points that resonated with me was the misguided instinct to do everything that clients ask. Being all things to all people is a recipe for disaster. In the remodeling business, examples abound. Clients ask if you can do repair work, very small jobs, when there is no system to handle those projects profitability because the company's real forte is large remodeling jobs.

What does a remodeling company owner typically think when such a call comes in and the current workload is light? "I have to keep my people busy." By falling into that trap, the business has become distracted from doing what it does best. And when distracted you may not be available or prepared when the right jobs come along.

I learned that straying from a process that works is risky, that results are what matter most, and that defining results is how you discover the process that works.

What does your company do well? What is your system for doing those projects? What can you do to get more such projects? For starters you can turn down work that doesn't fit, isn't profitable, or just doesn't feel right. That's hard to do for the typical people pleaser that most remodelers are and I was during the early years of our company.

How can you identify what your company does best? Set aside some time to reflect on it. Ask your employees, best clients, and trusted trade contractors. Look for the patterns. Remember that in all things—hiring, estimating, measuring—slowing down is often the best way to go fast.

CHAPTER 16

Exit Strategies

T HE IDEAL TIME TO THINK about selling your remodeling business is the day you start it. But that's not the way things work in real life. Unless you grew up in the business, inherited it, or got into it by some other opportunity, most of us started out swinging a hammer.

Now, decades later, you're slowing down, the kids are out of the house, the business is healthy, and you're ready to receive the reward for all that hard work by selling it to someone else. That sounds easy enough, but for most owners that's not the way things work in real life. Unless you've been planning for this day for years, you may find the business is worth the net value of its assets minus debts and nothing more. What's missing is equity—that mythical number that represents compensation for the risk you took, the sacrifices you made when times were lean, and the value of your company's reputation.

Planning For Life After Business

The world doesn't need another book about how to sell your small business. The reason I wanted to write *this* book is because remodeling isn't like most small businesses. Also, our experience was not like most remodelers' experience. Nina and I learned through trial and error to make our remodeling business work for us and how to build a profitable brand that had tangible equity.

As a result, we were able to sell our business in 2007 for enough money to be able to retire to a home we'd bought and had fully and meticulously renovated, and to continue taking our adventurous vacations. You could say we were lucky. The housing bubble was just about to burst, so we dodged a bullet. A year later, the economy was in the tank, the value of our building had diminished, and the industry was getting hammered. I doubt we'd have found any interest.

You could also say we were prepared to be lucky. We were able to sell when the time was right because we'd spent a decade planning for it. We started that part of our journey in 1998 when we invested in hiring a business consultant to help us get focused on strategic planning—the big picture.

She listened to Nina and me as we described our respective relationships to the business. Nina's was practical. It provided for our family. She had other interests that she wanted to be able to pursue. My relationship vacillated between all-consumed and overwhelmed. My family name was on all the trucks and signage. It was a matter of personal pride. But I was also getting tired of working all the time. And there were other interests I had thought about pursuing.

In the end, we decided to set a date by which we would be living a life free of our remodeling company, whether or not we were able to sell. Nina wanted to be out in five years.

That was way too short for me. In the end we agreed to a date ten years in the future. To me that was comfortably theoretical. I couldn't comprehend that far ahead so I didn't feel threatened by it.

But it turned out that setting the date—making that commitment—changed the way we related to the business. We now had a shared sense of purpose: to make sure that for the next ten years the business would earn what we felt we would need to sustain us in our retirement, and to take the steps that might attract a buyer. As I mentioned earlier, one of the long-term goals Nina and I had was to travel internationally before our twenty-fifth wedding anniversary. We did in 2000 and got the travel bug. I decided I didn't want to wait until I was older and possibly limited by health. I wanted to see the world.

Building A Brand

To make all this happen, my first assignment was to get better at selling our projects at a higher margin. We became more discerning about projects and clients. We began to track everything that worked and everything that didn't work, adjusting our systems and processes as we went. We wrote everything down and ended up with a road map of documents that would guide our employees in our absence.

That allowed us to take real vacations, eventually being away from the business as long as three weeks at a stretch. By the time we sold the company, we were working in the business no more than nine months of the year and had socked away what we felt we needed for retirement. It may seem counterintuitive that the way to prepare your business for sale is to go away. As it turns out, that flexibility made the company more attractive.

One of the most valuable things we did was participate in a peer group, first with Business Networks and then Remodelers Advantage. Twice a year about ten of us—noncompeting contractors from the US and Canada—met to share our successes, get feedback about how to address problems, and even share our financials. To see how we were doing relative to others was instructive and inspiring.

The key principles we followed were: focus on making a healthy profit rather than winning awards; build a brand by making us more visible; and build lives outside of work that would make it easier when the time came to let go. On the operating side, we followed the advice of Remodelers Advantage president Victoria Downing: assemble a management team of superstars; use systems throughout the business so that the team can run the business without you; and put together a sales bench that also doesn't depend on the owner.

"Remodeling companies that sell for high value have these things in common," Ms. Downing wrote in an article for the website Remodelers Advantage. However, "I've been in the business for over twenty years and can still count on my fingers the number of companies that have been sold successfully."

There's no road map for building a remodeling company brand, but there are a few things that we learned by trying or discovered the value of later. For example, researchers who authored the article "Eponymous Entrepreneurs" for the June 2017 issue of the *American Economic Review* found that companies named for the owner, like ours, had a return on assets almost double those that weren't. It turns out that when your name is on the door, you work a little harder to build and maintain a good reputation.

Paying It Forward Pays Back

In addition to the typical marketing a remodeling company does, we tried some other tactics with the goal of positioning us as a preferred provider. I wrote a column for the real estate section of a group of free newspapers that were delivered to communities in which we wanted to work.

Nina had joined a small group of contractors after the Berkeley Hills/Oakland fire of 1991 who put together a pamphlet of information for people whose homes had been damaged or destroyed. It was a comprehensive explanation of the process involved in getting their new home planned, permitted, and rebuilt. As a result of her involvement, she was asked to write a column for a local monthly periodical that was distributed to the areas in which we wanted to work.

Both Nina and I wrote for different national publications geared toward remodeling contractors. We were interested in making the industry more professional, and we wanted to be viewed as experts by our peers and vendors so they might refer us if the occasion came up. I spoke at our local chapter of the National Association of the Remodeling

Industry (NARI), sharing our insights and experience. In 2000, I began facilitating Remodelers Advantage roundtable meetings for other peer groups.

As Nina and I became active in the industry nationally, we began traveling to conferences and other events, giving feedback to other owners. That put me on a path that led to being elected president of NARI for the 2005–06 year.

By consciously creating lives that took us out of our day-to-day business routine, we became less dependent on the company for our sense of identity.

In spite of being preoccupied or unavailable for much of that year, we had done such a good job of setting up the company to operate without us that it was our best year ever.

Turning Over The Keys

By consciously creating lives that took us out of our day-to-day business routine, we became less dependent on the company for our sense of identity. That freedom gave us permission to sell.

As I pointed out at the beginning of this chapter, without planning, most remodeling companies end up being worth no more than their physical assets minus debt. In our case, one of those assets was the building we had owned for more than fifteen years instead of paying rent on an office. Not only had it grown in value, but owning it also made the company more attractive to the bankers who the buyer went to for financing. The buyer also liked the fact that the business address and phone number would stay the same.

All of these elements added value to the company, although we wouldn't find out how much until we actually sold the business.

During the decade that we shaped the business with the goal of being able to sell it, we weighed every decision in the context of the big picture, our plan. There were several important questions I tried to keep in the front of my mind as mentioned in Chapter 14:

- What do I want to be doing in my business?
- What don't I want to be doing in my business?
- How many hours a week am I willing to work in my business?
- How many weeks a year do I want to be doing something other than working on my business?
- What do I want to be doing when I'm not working in my business?
- What do I want my business to pay me in salary and benefits so I can take time off or pursue other interests?
- How much net profit will my business need to generate to do that?

In other words, how do I make sure my business is working for me, supporting what I want out of life, and not the other way around?

In the end, the most important bit of advice I would give anyone in our business is to find community. You're not in this alone. Everybody who is doing what you're doing is having the same or similar problems. Avoid isolating yourself. Connect with your peers, listen to your instincts, learn to be methodical, make a plan, and then stick to it.

The day we handed over the keys to the new owner of Winans Construction was emotional but also exhilarating. I took great satisfaction in leaving behind a well-run company with a reliable and professional staff, a full book of business, a legacy of first-class work, and thirty years of experience that I have used ever since to help other remodelers.

Acknowledgements

This book was able to be written because of the care and attention of many people over the course my life. Without their contributions, the book would never have come to be. I apologize to those whom I overlook mentioning here.

My mother and father instilled in me a desire to be of service to others. They gave so much of themselves to many people and organizations. I wish they could see this book, because so much of it reflects the lessons they taught me.

Our children, Paul, Bret, and Ben Winans, worked with us at different times in our respective lives. It was wonderful when they did. And I learned a lot from those experiences together.

Steve Nichols and I worked together on projects over the years. The way Steve ran his company set a standard that I measured myself against. He connected me with my first regular column opportunity. I am grateful for his confidence in me.

My peer group members in both BN5 at Business Networks and Mentor 1 at Remodelers Advantage (RA) provided needed insights and perspective that helped me become more the person I wanted to be instead of staying "who I am." Your input was sometimes hard to hear, and I am glad you provided it to me.

Penny Braun has been an unending source of encouragement. Penny helped me drive the book past obstacle after obstacle.

Linda Case and Victoria Downing asked me to be a facilitator of RA Roundtable meetings years ago. This work enabled me to help others get out of their own way, something that has brought me much satisfaction, and friends all over the US, Canada, and beyond. Your confidence in me is something I will never take for granted.

Sal Alfano suggested I write a blog once a week. That was 10 years ago. Most of the material this book is based on came from those many blog posts. Sal's gentle push was what got it all started. Without that push...

The contributions of R. Foster Winans and Chris Molé were very, very helpful in bringing the book to life. Their input and suggestions, offered over many months and years, made the difference. I cannot thank them enough.

Finally, Nina Winans, having provided gentle encouragement and the assistance as needed throughout my life, made the difference as I worked on the book. Without your help it would never have come to be.

Books Referenced

Collins, Jim. *Good To Great: Why Some Companies Make the Leap…and Others Don't.* HarperBusiness, a Division of HarperCollins Publishers: 2001.

Covey, Stephen R. *The 7 Habits of Highly Effective People: Powerful Lessons in Personal Change.* A Fireside Book, Simon & Schuster: 1989.

Daniels, David, MD, and Price, Virginia, PhD, *The Essential Enneagram: The Definitive Personality Test and Self-Discovery Guide.* Harper San Francisco, A Division of HarperCollins Publishers: 2000.

Francis, Linda Leigh. *Run Your Business So It Doesn't Run You: Create More Money, Time, and Fun!* Borah Press: 2000.

Gerber, Michael. *The E-Myth: Why Most Small Businesses Don't Work and What To Do About It.* HarperBusiness, a Division of HarperCollins Publishers: 1986.

Lencioni, Patrick. *The Five Dysfunctions of a Team: A Leadership Fable.* Jossey-Bass, a Wiley Company: 2002.

Mornell, Pierre, Dr. *45 Effective Ways for Hiring Smart! How to Predict Winners and Losers in the Incredibly Expensive People-Reading Game.* Ten Speed Press: 1998.

Ritchey, Tom and Axelrod, Alan. *I'm Stuck, You're Stuck: Break Through to Better Work Relationships and Results by Discovering Your DiSC Behavioral Style.* Berrett-Koehler Publishers, Inc: 2002.

Warrillow, John. *Built To Sell: Creating a Business That Can Thrive Without You.* Portfolio/Penguin: 2010.

Wickman, Gino. *Traction: Get A Grip On Your Business.* Benbella: 2011.

Additional Resources

Beckwith, Harry. *Selling The Invisible: A Field Guide to Modern Marketing.* Warner Books: 1997.

Blanchard, Kenneth, Oncken Jr., William, and Burrows, Hal. *The One Minute Manager Meets the Monkey.* Quill: 1989.

Booker, Kim and Doyle, Chip. *Selling To Homeowners the Sandler Way: A Proven Process for Selling Products and Services to Consumers in Their Home.* Sandler Training: 2015.

Burlingham, Bo. *Small Giants: Companies That Choose to Be Great Instead of Big.* Portfolio, The Penguin Group: 2005.

Carnegie, Dale. *How To Win Friends & Influence People.* Pocket Books; 1936.

Case, Linda and Downing, Victoria. *Mastering the Business of Remodeling: An Action Plan for Profit, Progress and Peace of Mind.* Remodelers Advantage: 2007.

Frankl, Viktor E. *Man's Search For Meaning: An Introduction to Logotherapy.* Touchstone: 1959.

Hill, Napoleon. *Think and Grow Rich.* Fawcett Columbine: 1937.

Kelly, Matthew. *The Dream Manager.* Beacon Publishing: 2007.

Kramers, Kraig. *CEO Tools: The Nuts-n-Bolts of Business for Every Manager's Success.* Gandy Dancer Press: 2002.

Meyer, Danny. *Setting the Table: The Transforming Power of Hospitality in Business.* HarperCollins Publishers: 2006.

Miller, John G. *QBQ!: The Question Behind the Question: What to Really Ask Yourself to Eliminate Blame, Complaining, and Procrastination.* QBQ, Inc.: 2004.

Patterson, Kerry, Grenny, Joseph, McMillan, Ron, and Switzler, Al. *Crucial Conversations: Tools for Talking When Stakes Are High.* McGraw-Hill: 2002.

Pausch, Randy. *The Last Lecture.* Hyperion: 2008.

Pollan, Stephen and Levine, Mark. *Die Broke: A Radical, Four-Part Financial Plan.* HarperBusiness: 1997.

Prager, Dennis: *Happiness Is A Serious Problem: A Human Nature Repair Manual.* ReganBooks: 1998.

Sewell, Carl and Brown, Paul. *Customers for Life: How to Turn That One-Time Buyer into a Lifetime Customer.* A Currency Book: 1990.

Stack, Jack with Burlingham, Bo. *The Great Game of Business.* A Currency Paperback: 1992.

Tannen, PhD, Deborah. *You Just Don't Understand: Women and Men in Conversation.* Ballentine Books: 1990.

About the Author

An internationally recognized leader in the remodeling industry, **Paul L. Winans** has been sharing his feet-on-the-ground experiences with other business owners for more than 30 years. In addition to executive and team consulting, Paul is a writer and a popular, sought-after speaker. Paul is a past president of the National Association of the Remodeling Industry and was recognized as one of 15 Remodeling Innovators of the past 30 years upon *Qualified Remodeler* magazine's 30th anniversary. Paul and his wife, Nina, sold their award-winning remodeling company in 2007, its impeccable reputation, staff, systems, and procedures being key attractors and factors in the successful transition.

Please visit www.winansconsulting.com
for more information.

Made in United States
Troutdale, OR
06/26/2023

10816298R00086